Hannah

Hannah

by **Hannah Westberg** edited by Deborah Reber

Health Communications, Inc.
Deerfield Beach, Florida

www.hcibooks.com

Library of Congress Cataloging-in-Publication Data

Westberg, Hannah.
    My true story of drugs, cutting, and mental illness / by
    Hannah Westberg.
        p. cm.
    ISBN-13: 978-0-7573-1528-2
    ISBN-10: 0-7573-1528-3
    1. Westberg, Hannah—Mental health.   2. Multiple personality in
    children—Patients—United States—Biography.   I. Title.
    RJ506.M84W47 2010
    618.92'852360092—dc22
    [B]

                                                        2010023156

Publisher: Health Communications, Inc.
            3201 S.W. 15th Street
            Deerfield Beach, FL 33442–8190

Cover design by Larissa Hise Henoch
Interior formatting by Dawn Von Strolley Grove

To Aniko Becsei, Erin Bray, and Augusten Burroughs

Contents

This is the story of a girl

This is the story of a girl whose life so far has been a series of regrets and near misses.

This is the story of a girl who realized in the middle of writing her story that her problems can't be explained by depression alone.

This is the story of a girl who decided to accept the stigmatized diagnosis of borderline personality disorder (BPD) so that she can recover from it.

This is the story of a girl who refuses to be defined solely by her mental illness.

Beginnings

I FOUND OUT THE EXTENT to which my childhood was fucked up when I began writing this book. I thought my bed-wetting, inappropriate anger, stealing, and running away were just quirks . . . that I was a bad seed. Of course, my mother's strange upbringing, childhood trauma, and abusive first husband could've only led to horrible things. Nobody could have gone through what she did and emerge unscathed.

Even as I sit down to write, I'm not quite sure how to approach my childhood memories. Perhaps as the bomb squad approaches a mysterious package: tentatively, as if any little touch might set off an explosion. But I'll just dive in. Everything that could explode already has—I just have to watch out for sparks as I clean up the mess left behind. Okay, it's not as if my childhood was so tragic. There was no big trauma. Just a lot of mess. I'll start at the beginning.

My mother met her first husband, George, at an Alcoholics Anonymous (AA) meeting when she was nineteen. George, however, was not attending the meeting—he was merely waiting outside and drinking. He married and impregnated her soon after. He was always taking out loans and never repaying them. He was always on the run from the law and wanted in different states for unpaid speeding tickets and DUIs. He had moved my mother and my brother, Nevada, to Reno to flee his latest charges.

From what I've heard, he was the classic abuser of both my mother and my brother. He would get drunk and beat my mom. He would flick my baby brother in the head, swing him around in a terrifying way. He would watch hardcore porn in front of my toddler brother. He would drive drunk with baby Nevada in the front seat. His crazy roommate shot him in the leg, right past my mother, past Nevada's playpen. My mother finally left him, but before they could get divorced, he was murdered—handcuffed to a tree and shot by one of the people he'd ripped off, of which there were many.

My father is George's brother, and though his childhood wasn't much better than my mother's, his mental health was. The first sign that his marriage to my mom wouldn't last was that they met in AA. They fell in love, ignored codependency issues, and quickly became engaged. My father adopted Nevada when my brother was still young, and for a while, the three of them looked like the picture-perfect family. Mom converted to Catholicism and they were active in the church. Dad introduced her to the pro-life movement and she became obsessed with it. She used breast-feeding and the rhythm method as the only acceptable forms of birth control. As a result, she had my sister Sarah when Nevada was seven, Rachel three years later, and me two years after that.

While we were kids, my mom became increasingly manic, but not in totally destructive ways. She held down a job and raised four children, always being tender and loving to each one of us. She gave us baby massages, sang Bob Dylan, took us to the park and the library. She carried me to the hospital when I got chicken pox in my throat and got dehydrated. She lived for her children. This only spurred on her pro-life activism. She would stay up all night writing letters and articles.

She received local fame for her feminist pro-life stance and her graphic drawings of third-term abortions. She was arrested more than once for protesting outside abortion clinics. She believed more and more that she was on a mission from God. Once, during a bad ice storm, she got into the car, convinced that she had to go to city hall to get the floor plans of an abortion clinic in town. When her organization started advocating the murder of abortionists, she left, but she shifted her mania elsewhere.

She stopped sleeping with my father. She had never enjoyed sex. It either reminded her of obligation sex with her abusive first husband or of the gang rape she experienced as a teen. After four children, she couldn't handle the emotional burden any longer. She nearly wiped out their savings. According to Mom, she made random purchases that she couldn't keep track of, but Dad had suspicions that she spent it on prescription medications, which she was abusing. She started drinking again. One time she got drunk, decided that she had to leave us, and got into the car. Her mother hung on to the car, trying to stop her, and she dragged Grandma behind her.

She starved herself down to ninety pounds. She tried to kill herself in different ways, mainly by overdosing. Eventually, she sought help. At first she went to an unlicensed Catholic psychiatrist who diagnosed demon possession in my mother. After the exorcism supposedly failed, the psychiatrist told my mother she couldn't see her anymore. Mom was devastated. She truly believed she was hopelessly possessed because she didn't know what else to believe.

Eventually, she was given the correct diagnosis: schizoaffective disorder. This was after being treated for alcoholism, anorexia-bulimia, suicidality, and manic depression, all things that were symptoms of the disorder. Schizoaffective combines the mania and depression of bipolar disorder and the psychosis of schizophrenia. On top of that, my dad was suffering from depression and couldn't take care of her.

It's about this time when my first memory comes in. I was two years old. My sisters and I waited outside the kitchen and watched as our parents screamed at each other. I didn't care. I wanted some chips. I walked into the kitchen, even though my sisters tried to stop me.

"You stole my wallet!"

"Well, you stole my wallet!"

I tugged at my mother's shirt. "Mommy, I want chips!" She didn't look down.

My parents divorced when I was three or four. They split up because my mother thought she could better handle her job, her mental illness, and raising children without the added burden of being a wife. People generally believe this situation is more emotionally scarring for me than if my parents had waited to split up until I was older. Truth be told, I don't have enough conscious memories of them as a couple to mourn anything. They just weren't meant to last and I'm cool with that. The aftermath was chaotic, but I'm pretty sure I would've ended up the problem child anyway.

I believe I was four years old when my mom put us into a cab and sent us to our grandparents so she could admit herself into the psych ward the first time. I've lost track of how many times she's done it since.

Meanwhile, my dad lived with his parents for a short time and then in a studio apartment. When my mother served him with divorce papers at his work, he was surprised. Some might say furious. Others might say he had abandoned us, but that doesn't explain the tumultuous custody battle that followed.

My grandparents hated him before and they've hated him since. They did everything they could to keep us away from him, and covered for mom at the same time. By this time, she had been in and out of different hospitals and our grandparents took care of us for up to a month at a time. When Mom was in the hospital, they would take my sisters to school and me to preschool. They would pick me up and take me to their house, where I would watch children's shows and eat ice cream while sitting on the dishwasher. They would pick up my sisters and we would play dress-up or play with Legos. When Mom wasn't in the hospital, my grandparents would take us to her house in the evening when she got home from work. They did their best to shield us from everything.

The divorce got nasty. Mom accidentally brought up her mental health, and then Dad and his lawyer got full access to her psychiatric files. He moved into a slightly bigger apartment and got visitation rights. Once, before his visit was over, Mom showed up to kidnap us, with Grandpa driving the getaway car. When Dad's lawyer found out, it was over for

Mom. Dad got full custody. From then on, we would only see Mom from noon on Saturdays to 6 PM on Sundays. Eventually, holidays were divided up between my parents, and she got us for two weeks in the summer, that is, when she wasn't in the hospital.

Since my mother's mental illness was such a huge part of my childhood, I have pleasant memories attached to it. I remember some social worker taking my sister and me out for ice cream, asking questions to determine if she was a fit mother. We were baffled and eager for acceptance, so we told him what we thought he wanted to hear. I'm sure my sister Rachel knew it was about keeping our mother, but I was in it for the ice cream.

I remember visiting my mom in the hospital and playing dirty-word Boggle before I was old enough to know many dirty words. Nevada tried to make our visits to the hospital into fun outings. When I was older, it was my turn to bring comfort. I would bring my mom a Starbucks drink with an order so long only I could remember it—Iced Venti Sugar-Free Vanilla Nonfat Latte No Whip. She, in turn, would make me crafts, like bracelets with letter beads that spelled out H-BOMB, ROTFLMAO, and FAUX HIP. We got through the visits with inappropriate humor. We laughed way too much when mom had the energy to feign happiness.

Of course, I have bad memories, too. It was hard to have so many victims and no one to blame. My siblings were too young to protect me, except for Nevada, who had his hands full protecting Mom. My dad was doing his best being a single parent with three girls, struggling with his own depression. My mom loved us boundlessly and couldn't help being in the grips of mental illness. Could I be mad at the doctors who used her as a guinea pig? The Catholic psychiatrist who convinced her she was possessed? Could I track down every person who had traumatized her and then beat them up? It wouldn't help. She's her own worst enemy. I can't be mad at her mood swings or the voices in her head.

Mostly, my mother was sedated, smoking, drinking diet soda and instant coffee, and reading thousands of books and magazines. Her life had accelerated the aging process. I dyed her gray hair. Bulimia, most likely, confined her to dentures in her forties. Her medication combo often left her as an empty shell, nearly incapable of staying awake. She had to wear a diaper because she was paralyzed by her nighttime pills and couldn't move, much less make it to the bathroom. She wasn't a real person to me for years.

My dad was in a deep depression before, during, and after the divorce. Typically he was unable to get out of bed, and my sisters and I would run wild. My sisters picked on me mercilessly, and I did my best to fight back, but I would only end up throwing fruitless tantrums, acting out, and getting punished for it. My older sister, Sarah, resented being our babysitter, so she took the position literally. When I was especially bad, she would sit on me, or shut me in a closet. This only made me angrier, but it was better than Dad's form of punishment. He took spanking to the extreme. I wasn't the type of child to willingly bend over his knee and take it, so he had to chase after me, screaming and hitting me in the area of my butt. He threatened with a belt or a shoe, but only spanked with an open hand while I was running and crying. He had no other way to deal with me. I was out of control.

Once, while we were putting away dishes, Rachel started picking on me. I snapped and grabbed a knife and started jabbing at her. She held a bunch of mugs by the handles for defense, but the knife slipped through two of them and stabbed her finger. Blood dripped to the floor and I started bawling. She told me to be quiet and clean up the blood. Neither of us wanted to incur the wrath of Dad. She was in the bathroom rinsing off her finger when he came down the stairs, demanding to know what was going on. I wailed, "I stabbed her!"

He screamed, *"You stabbed her?!"* Rachel came in the room to show him that I only meant in the finger, but that didn't stop his screaming.

Another time, Rachel and her friend were picking on me at the bus stop and I decided to go back home. I hated my second grade teacher, anyway, and would fake stomachaches to get out of school. When my dad called down the stairs to check if anyone was home, I sneaked out the back door so I wouldn't get caught and sent to school. I hid in the backyard while people searched and police were called. It only got harder and harder to reveal myself. I had tried running away before, but this time they assumed I had been kidnapped. I finally showed myself and saw my dad cry for the first time.

This is the type of thing my dad's girlfriend, Carol, walked into. The place was a mess. My sisters and I looked like ragamuffins, and I would barely eat anything. Because I was a picky eater, I was deathly pale with dark circles under my eyes. Carol had no tolerance for this. She bought us clothes, cleaned our rooms, taught us manners, gave us chores, and reprimanded us. She had a hard time dealing with our not knowing certain things, and so we got lectured a lot. It didn't help that she didn't ask for this burden, didn't even want children, but she also led my Brownie troop, took us to Disneyland, and choreographed my dance to *Fame* in the talent show. She taught us songs, took me to dance class, and we drew pictures for each other. She was strict, yes, but our family also considered her a godsend.

My dad told me he broke up with Carol at Chuck E. Cheese one day with little explanation. They got back together a few months later and every almost-breakup thereafter, according to him, was because Carol wanted out. If my memory serves me, the first fight they ever had was about me, as most of their fights have been since. Dad would scream, throw things, slam doors, and knock things over. Carol would mostly just cry and leave. In later years, she would vent to me, convincing me that my father was abusing her. I wasn't totally comfortable with my role of ventee, and there were other times I felt that maybe I was receiving too much information, like the time she reminded my siblings and me that she'd had her tubes tied because she never wanted kids. She would say our reluctance to do our chores was proof that we didn't love her and we wanted her gone. Even when we all moved in together when I was nine, she didn't sell her old house for years in case she ever wanted to go back; at least that's the way I interpreted it. After a screaming match with my dad or me, she would get into her car and drive off without telling us where she was going. She would cool down for a few hours or stay at a friend's house, or worse, start packing. She never moved out . . . I think she just like knowing she had the option.

Unfortunately, I didn't have any options. My mom was who she was. She would always do the best she could, even when it wasn't good enough. My dad and Carol were together, for better or worse, and her threats of abandoning me were real and left their mark. At the end of the day, this was my family, my history, my legacy. And it would impact the way my life would unfold in ways I never could have imagined.

Corrupted

SH-DOOBY DOOBY DOOBY DOOTIN' DOO WAH, dah
doo, doo doo doo dootin' doo wah, bop bop sh-dooby dooby dootin'
doo wah, dwee dwee dwee bop dootin' da tah doo wah.

This is what I was supposed to do. And I couldn't handle it.

I was awarded a scatting solo at an eighth grade choir concert. I've always been comfortable performing in front of
large groups, as long as that performance didn't involve
singing. I had been praised for my scatting in auditions and
rehearsals, but the fact that I was going to be doing it in front
of so many people brought about a physical nervousness that
was unbearable. Of course, it might have been bearable had
I not recently learned to solve any amount of stress by dip-
ping into my Altoids tin of other people's medications.

Before the concert, I was shaky, foggy, and weak. There was a sour, twisted feeling in my stomach. I took one brown pill. I felt better. I had no idea what this or any other pill was. I later discovered that it was Thorazine, an antipsychotic that's known to heavily sedate its users. I took two more and I started to fade.

It was like nothing I've ever felt naturally. I couldn't keep my body awake, never mind alert. I shook and slapped myself, splashed cold water on my face, and laid ice cubes over my eyes. My vision had narrowed as if I was wearing horse blinders. I didn't know the uppers from the downers, so another pill might floor me. I left, my head drooping, eyelids falling, and jolting myself upright every few seconds.

I had managed to stay standing during two songs, very close to falling off the back of the risers throughout. Two great fears had cruelly united; fear of singing in front of an audience and fear of dying.

It was time for my solo. I stood in front of the microphone. The eager faces of the crowd were hazy. The loud jazz suddenly turned into tinkling carnival sounds. I could have sworn my choir teacher was off the beat and playing all the wrong notes. I couldn't do what I had practiced so fervently. My flat and tired voice blurted out sh-dooby-doobies. I had to stay awake for at least a few more bars. I had to keep from fainting. I made it through and passed out in my choir robe at home. I stayed awake just long enough. This was a curse; I had to wait longer to bottom out.

I find it astounding how much what I initially used for control took over and destroyed me. I stole from the medicine cabinet, my depressed father, my ADD sister, and my stepmother who was suffering from pain. Worst of all, I was stealing from my psychiatric-guinea pig mother's candy mix of pharmaceuticals. I would scrounge and save them all, find fistfuls whenever I looked through my room. At the end, I was practically leaving a trail of them. I never knew what would happen. Nights awake, mind racing, pulling my hair out. Sick and scratching, thirsty and scared, once paranoid to the point of using the litter box. I popped a handful before a test and passed out on the desk between the multiple choice and essay questions. Sometimes it made me stupid. I passed out for days at a time.

I started grinding them up and snorting them. Trying to

make the high better, trying my best to reach a reprieve of all emotions. Little piles of white powder and straws cut into thirds defined my life. It burned in my nose, brightened my head. This was the method I used when I was especially desperate. I was trying to channel the cokehead inside me, as if snorting it made it more serious, more believable than prescriptions. It hit me faster, especially the uppers, when I couldn't stand that dragging pull of life. I was looking for any way out of my mind. My connection was my fucked-up family.

Ultimately, my parents locked up every medication, prescribed or over-the-counter. But I still found access. All I sought out was an escape from consciousness, insecurities, and maybe reality. Instead, my addiction made every day a horror story.

But popping pills wasn't enough. I had another vice, another form of escape . . . cutting. As illogical as it sounds, my cutting used to be logical. I would do something wrong, feel stupid, hear or read about something bad happening somewhere in the world, and then I would blame myself and believe I deserved punishment for it. I thought if I atoned for my wrongdoings, the universe would be in balance again.

My therapist told me to recognize the natural consequences that already exist. The universe balances itself without my controlling it: I don't turn in the assignment, my grade goes down. That is the punishment. I don't need to cut. This worked for a while. But what if there is no natural consequence? And what if this habit turns into addiction, something that can't be reasoned away?

The first time I cut myself I was in the seventh grade. I don't remember why. I don't remember what could have possibly prompted me to slice my skin open. But I do remember what the scissors looked like. I remember how it felt when I first dragged the blade across my wrist.

The last time I cut was two weeks ago. I vowed it would be the last time. But then I count the scars on my arms and remember that that's about how many times I've vowed to stop before.

I honestly can't remember how I knew about cutting. The entire concept of self-mutilation seems alien to most people. It would still be a few years for emo to become trendy. I was only slightly aware of cutting outside of the context of suicide. How I came to the conclusion to use this coping mechanism is beyond me. It just made sense to do it for punishment, for balance . . . later for plain comfort. And if I hit a vein, that was an added bonus.

I had no sense of covering it up at first. Cutting began as a surprising one- or two-time deal. Hiding didn't seem like a real obstacle, not with an irritable cat in the house. I had no idea it would become a habit and concealing it would become an activity in and of itself. I started at the beginning of my forearm, at the elbow. I began deepening the original cut. I slipped an X-Acto knife into my sleeve and went into the school bathroom. I cut as much as I could bear, rolled down my sleeve, and walked back to class. Eventually, I had a few gaping wounds on my arms.

On our way to choir, my friend Lizzy grabbed my arm to get my attention. I sort of yelped.

"What? What is it? Let me see your arm."

"No, forget it."

"Does your mom hit you?"

"What? No!"

She hounded me all through lunch. Desperate to get her

off my back, and probably for some validation, I showed her.

She gasped. "Hannah, what the hell? These are huge."

"So what? You cut."

"That's not the same. I just have little baby slices from where my friends and I were making cool scars. Yours are really serious."

"Whatever, hypocrite."

Who was she to be passing judgment? She was just one of my bad influences. She and Ray, Erica, Kerry, and Sam were the first to introduce me to self-destructive behaviors. Seventh and eighth grade were all about skipping class, cutting, and popping pills. I once pissed into a condom so Lizzy could pass her drug test. Lizzy and Kerry were both beaten by their fathers. Ray's mom dealt pot. Erica was murdered at a party when she was fourteen. Kerry and Sam were pregnant by the time they were eighteen. Sam cut herself, too. These were my idols. These were my best friends.

Sam, Ray, and I had become friends on the Excel bus. We lived near a middle school that didn't offer gifted courses, so we took the bus to the middle school that did. Sam corrupted me and I loved her for it. She was a year older, and radically accept that it was a long journey. I followed a Pilates tape and jogged on my dad's garage sale elliptical. I did so happily. I made my social gatherings more about activity and less about food. I substituted side salads for French fries and quit drinking Guava Rockstars. Instead of desserts, I ate Boston cream pie-flavored lite yogurt. Instead of chips, fat-free saltines. All of my TV dinners could be switched for low-calorie ones. Everything decadent had a healthy counterpart. I eventually cut out cows, pigs, and soda. I lost forty-five pounds. More and more pants became too big, and older pants began to fit.

Today, my food issues are far from solved. I still slip up, from emotional eating to emotional not-eating. But I try to find joy in my little accomplishments and in being healthy. I try to allow myself some wiggle room and that seems to help me to keep going.

because she thought I was cool, I got to hang out in the back of the bus with the badass eighth graders. They talked about getting fucked up and partying, and I tried to keep up. I had fun, even though Sam was the only one who was nice to me. I wasn't trying to fall in with the bad crowd; I was trying to be accepted.

I met Ray in the middle of the bus with the nerdy kids. We bonded over pure silliness before we bonded over drugs. I envied her confidence. I envied her boots. The first day of sixth grade, she was dressed in post-punk gear.

"So you're into punk?" I said.

"Yeah," she said.

"Joey Ramone: dead or alive?"

"Who?"

Despite this start, she turned out to be really cool. She led us on for thirty minutes with a made-up story about her stay in the psych ward. We tried to trip her up by asking more and more questions.

"How did you get in there?"

"My mom found me blacking out the eyes of all my Barbie dolls, so she took me in."

"So how do you tongue your meds?"

"You put them in the space between your cheek and your lower teeth—they check under the tongue."

"You learned how to pick a lock? How?"

"You take a bobby pin and a needle and jiggle them around until you hear a click."

Then she got off the bus, laughing at how gullible we were. I was impressed.

Ray became my best friend, but Sam was my mentor. She was a huge badass. She had done everything and seen it all. Being a self-destructive druggie gave me a group to fit into and an outlet for my undiagnosed depression. Now, in addition to cutting and popping pills alone, I was getting drunk and high with friends. I passed along my good pills and some cigarettes to Sam, Kerry, and Erica. The first time I ever smoked pot, I skipped school with Lizzy and Erica. They were the worst, the most neglected, the most headed for disaster.

At the beginning of ninth grade, Erica was found suffocated in a basement shower at a house party. The man responsible regularly threw drinking and drugging parties for neighborhood teens from my type of self-destructive crowd. I went to the funeral and saw her body, dressed in her choir clothes and made up in makeup she would never have worn. I saw all the people who left her at that party and probably passed the guilt to someone else to get by. I saw her mother, whom I had only seen once before, screaming and crying at the coffin. My friends and I stood together, drying our eyes and swapping Erica stories, convincing ourselves that she would have wanted us to party in her memory.

At the start of freshman year, even though I had scars and not wounds, I couldn't reveal my arms at all, not even to my boyfriend. But by the end of the year, I wore short sleeves to school. My belief was that hiding the scars gave them more power. If I put them out there and let everyone get used to the scars, eventually they would no longer be noticed. If I hid them and someone happened to see the scars, they would be shocked and the scars would draw more attention and shame.

Today, I know that by showing them, I'm doing the opposite of showing off. I'm forcing them to be mundane. When people comment and ask if it's a cry for help or being emo, or if they try to share cutting stories with me in a positive way, I don't indulge them. I tell them the purpose of my sleeve length. I cover the scars when I go for job interviews or to see my Catholic grandparents, but mostly, when the weather is warm, they're out there. Faded scars prove that cutting is a part of my past and not my present. This became a lie when I relapsed and cut repeatedly on my upper thighs; however, my belief that cutting is bad hasn't changed. After I overcame my last relapse, I got a tattoo of a henna design that camouflages the scars and replaces them with something beautiful. It shows that I can and will turn my past for the better.

The Ward

THE PSYCH WARD IS WHERE YOU GO to get from fragile to shattered. It's like taking your car to get it washed and getting your windshield broken in the process. If my suicide attempt was cathartic at all, if it made me feel lucky to be alive, I wouldn't know. The will to live was beaten out of me before the drugs had time to pass through my system.

I didn't plan it. It just seemed natural. I had an Altoids tin filled with pills pilfered from my mom's stash. I was lying on my bed, with no proof that this emptiness would ever cease, and I placed the pills in lines on my stomach. Fifteen little maroon pills, five little yellow ones, and five little white ones. I knew from experience that the maroon ones knocked you out, but I didn't know what any of them were. I don't know why I chose them, the colors and quantity were random. I had plenty of pills still left in the tin. All I knew was that they meant release. They gave me a reprieve from life. I had been upping the amount for a while, so this much seemed all right. The prospect of accidentally dying seemed okay.

I slept. I slept for twenty-four hours. When I woke up, I didn't really wake up. I walked down the hall and fell down. My eyes wouldn't open, my legs wouldn't stand, my body wouldn't work. I forced myself up and walked a few more steps but fell down again. I collapsed on the downstairs couch. My parents attributed it to adolescent lethargy. I slept for another twelve hours.

When I woke up again, I woke up hard. I woke up screaming. My jaw was sliding to the left farther than it could go. I couldn't push it back. The pain was unbelievable. I felt my eyes rolling back into my head, I couldn't hold my head up, and I was moaning uncontrollably with every exhale. I felt like I was possessed.

The ER doctors immediately recognized an overdose, but it was too late to pump my stomach. I sat there with a needle in one arm pumping medicine in and a needle in the other arm pumping blood out. Dad and Carol looked on dis-approvingly, and the doctors called my mother in hopes of identifying what I took. Thorazine mostly, as it turns out, the notorious sedative.

They admitted me in the psych ward. I wasn't even allowed to go home and pack a bag. They tried to give me an initial interview, but my jaw slowly locked open. They gave me a Benadryl and told me to lie down in my room. My roommate entered. She was thin, with red hair and wearing a flannel shirt.

"Hi, I'm Shelby. I guess we're roommates."

I tried to say my name, but only managed, "Ine Anah."

She lay down on the bed next to mine. "Are you straight?"

Still out of it, unable to inquire why she asked, I answered, "Yeah . . . uh, yeah."

"Oh, because I'm bisexual. Sometimes people get uncom-fortable having a bisexual roommate."

My jaw had finally started closing. "No problem."

She came over to my bed. "So, have you ever thought about being with a girl, though?"

I giggled. The meds were kicking in, making my jaw loose

and my mind looser. "No. I mean, there's nothing wrong with experimentation, I guess, but I'm really only into guys."

She straddled me. "But how do you know if you've never tried girls?"

She held my shoulders down and kissed me. This was my first kiss. I weakly tried to push her away. She thought I was just being playful. I really wanted her off my bed, but the drugs that were still working their way through my system took away my strength. She rolled over next to me, spooning me. She placed my hand on her breast, and I pulled it back and tried to shove her off. She just bounced back and took my hand and gripped it against her breast again.

"Get off my bed!"

She laughed. "Oh, come on. Oh, shit, it's time for group."

She rushed out the door. I started sobbing.

At least this chaos filled the emptiness. I longed to be void of emotions again.

One of the rules in the psych ward was Absolutely No Touching, not even a high five. This was counterproductive on their part. The human touch is proven to be psychologically healing. The lack of touch affected me deeply. I cried six times the first day, and at least once a day after that. Of course, the one time the rule should have protected me, it wasn't enforced.

Another rule was No War Stories. I guess that referred to proudly sharing tales of self-destructiveness. We never followed this rule. People in this type of situation like to turn their pain into a competition. We got caught up comparing tragedies just to get some validation.

This mental one-upmanship doesn't take place only in the hospital. A year or two later when self-harm became cool, people expressed their jealousy at how big my scars were. I didn't appreciate this. I started wearing short sleeves so that if anyone accidentally got a peak at my scars, it wouldn't be a big deal. Exposing the scars took their power away. Everyone I saw regularly stopped noticing them. People still occasionally ask if I want attention, if I'm emo, how I did it, if I am suicidal. I tell them, "Wow, I didn't even notice these until you pointed them out."

In the psych ward, the doctors said I couldn't walk around in short sleeves because it might shock some of the younger patients who come in for, say, hallucinations. I took this to mean, "Put away your self-indulgent, adolescent excuse for mental illness and let the people with real problems get help."

I heard this statement in just about everything they said. The fellow patients were merciless because I was so sensitive. I couldn't stop crying. Being alienated for it didn't help the matter. The antidepressants they put me on weren't helping the matter, either.

I waited. I read my books. I painted. I played cards. I watched the instructional videos. I watched *Napoleon Dynamite* three times and country music video countdowns. I sneaked in a friend by passing her off as a cousin. I got caught, but I still got the Goldfish and mascara she brought me. I applied makeup in the cloudy metal mirror. I chastised the addiction counselor for not knowing anything. I dared her to back up her statistics. I tried to keep it cool in group and individual therapy. I was honest enough but nothing got accomplished. I took a placement test. One of the administrators told me that I scored higher than anyone else who had done all four "gateway drugs"—alcohol, pot, cigarettes, and huffing. I guess my brain wasn't totally dead. It was just my emotions that were decimated.

I waited. I smashed my clock and almost cut myself with the glass shards. My new roommate, who was also a pill popper, took them away and gave them to a doctor. I desperately missed the affirmation that time was passing. During the two-hour changing of the guard, when everyone was confined to their rooms, I would peak my head out and ask what time it was. They would bark at me to get back into my room. I read the graffiti on the walls.

They finally told me I was going to be placed in a long-term treatment facility. It was a rehabilitation center a few hours away for people with mental health issues.

"I can't spend six months in this Children's Farm Home place! I'm going into my freshman year of high school next month, and I haven't even gotten the summer reading."

"Hannah, this is ultimately about your mental health. School is not the priority—your life is."

I didn't want to prioritize my life if this is what it felt like. I wanted to go home and try to end it again. But I didn't have a say in the matter. This fact shaped my life, because the time I would spend at the Children's Farm Home was the best and the worst of my life. I thought I was going to a long-term version of the same psych ward hell. I was so wrong.

Whether you anticipate fortune or misfortune, it doesn't make sense to expect more of the same. Life doesn't work that way. I was along for the ride.

Rehab

DEAR REHAB, I TOOK THE LIBERTY of writing a slogan for you: "We will give you all the tools you need to deal with life inside of rehab."

Before I headed off to Children's Farm Home, I was allowed to go home and pack my bags. When I walked into my bedroom, I realized the desolation I had been living in. I'm a pretty messy person, and people with depression generally don't have the wherewithal to clean, but my room, seen through fresh eyes, looked unlivable. I couldn't see the floor because it was piled so high with clothes.

I threw some clothes into a duffel bag, not caring if they were clean or not. I tossed in some toiletries and an Altoids tin. I opened it to show my parents that it held, in fact, mints and not pills. The pills were in another tin, still somewhere in the room. My father offered to play the song he wrote for me while I was in the hospital, but I couldn't handle it. We played the Moody Blues soundtrack on our emotionally strained road trip down to Corvallis. The irony wasn't lost on me.

When we got there, the administrators had assessed my stay should last six months, but my insurance company would allow only twenty-eight days. I was surprised to hear the long and detailed history of mental illness in our family that my father provided. I was asked to give phone numbers of people whom my parents approved of my calling. I could think of only one, a girl from my group therapy whom I wasn't terribly close to.

We walked into the "cottage," which was really just a large house with a few alterations. The downstairs had two large main rooms, a kitchen, two offices, and a room where they kept the medicine and confiscated items. The upstairs had half a dozen rooms with two beds each, metal doors with little windows so the staff could check on us, and windows with alarms that would alert the staff if they were opened without permission. A large communal bathroom held three sinks, three stalls, and a shower area. The shower area included four showerheads and a tub that nobody used, but thankfully, we never had to shower more than one at a time. Another rule was that each person had to wear flip-flops in the shower to avoid spreading fungus. A girl who talked to her Barbies sang loud and off-key whenever she was in there.

The laundry room was in the basement, but other than that, the basement served no purpose. While I was at the rehab, the basement was an ongoing painting project. We would go down there and cover it with three different bright shades of purple. Supposedly, it was going to become a game room, but the only evidence of that was a single foosball table.

A basketball hoop was out back, along with a pool, a track, a school, and stables for equestrian therapy on the campus. Apparently, the center also offered archery, but I never saw it. In many ways, the Home was kind of like summer camp, with psychiatry being just one of the many activities. There was a main building with a clinic and administrative offices. Across the way stood the male equivalent of our cottage and another cottage for younger kids. In the middle of the campus was a gated and locked building that was for more serious cases. I once recognized someone I knew from the psych ward standing by that building. He called from the playground and I tried to respond to his greeting, but I was sternly told I wasn't allowed to talk to the people in there.

While my bags were searched, I met my roommate. She was a thirteen-year-old unapologetic anorexic. She had the number eleven written on her arm in ballpoint pen.

"What does eleven mean?"

"It represents two stick figures," she explained. "Anorexics use that number to get skinny. Eleven bites of food, eleven sit-ups, that sort of thing."

I was presented with a welcome basket. It had flip-flops, a journal, a teddy bear, and some starter toiletries. All I really wanted was a razor. My armpit hair had gotten long in my week and a half in the hospital. The boys in the ward said that the roll-on deodorant ripped their hair out, but it didn't work for me.

Along with the welcome basket, I got an extensive list of rules, the strangest being that you couldn't wear just a bathing suit in the pool, you had to wear a shirt and shorts over it.

Swimming was the first thing I did. I had to borrow a pair of shorts that some past patient had left behind. I didn't know any of these people and suddenly I was swimming with them. I swam to one end of the pool and back to prove to the lifeguard that I could be in the pool without drowning. Those who couldn't stayed in the shallow end. One girl noticed I was alone and approached me.

"So how did you get here, if you don't mind me asking?" I said.

"I got referred here from juvie. I was there on an assault charge."

"Who did you assault?"

"My mom. She was being a bitch and I hit her and she pressed charges."

"That sucks."

"Yeah."

As we walked back, I overheard her talking to a staff member. Apparently she had gone out drinking on her last home visit. When she got back to her room, she started blasting No Doubt's album *Tragic Kingdom*. This was a pleasant change from the "bitches and hos" rap my roommate liked to play.

I talked to my parents on the phone, and they sent packages and visited. I didn't really want them there. I got a God-filled letter from a relative my parents swore they wouldn't tell about what had happened. Having extended family know about my overdose just made me feel more guilty. What I did appreciate came from my brother, who was stationed in Iraq. He sent me books on Buddhism, an interest we shared, and a hilarious and encouraging letter with a picture he had taken of me at a college basketball game years earlier. When he was in college, he was always taking me and my sisters on outings, to parties, to concerts, and to do volunteer work. Now that he had graduated and was serving overseas, the contact had lessened and I missed him.

Back at the cottage, we had a group meeting. We didn't have group therapy—just meetings every morning and afternoon to announce what dialectical behavioral therapy (DBT) skill we were going to use that half of the day. DBT is a fantastic thing if you know how to use it. No one had bothered to teach it to me.

When we went around the room, my roommate always said she was going to use "Cheerleading," which is a simple skill wherein you affirm yourself throughout the day. You could tell she didn't care about the process, she just wanted to get home and starve herself to death.

"What skill are you going to practice today, Hannah?"

"I have no idea what any of this is."

He pointed to one of ten words on colorful construction paper stapled to the wall. "Why don't you do Ten Candles? I'll teach it to you later."

Ten Candles is basically self-guided meditation. You imagine you are in a room that is dark except for ten lit candles. They can be any kind of candles, anywhere in the room, arranged any way you like. Then you approach them, breathe in slowly through your nose, and with each exhale, you blow out the candles one by one until the room is dark. A lot of DBT concepts are similar to that of Buddhism, with which I was familiar. Meditation was fairly common but specific scenarios were not universal. Every DBT practitioner has their favorite kind. Ten Candles quickly became mine.

When we went to dinner, we first lined up at the door before we could leave. Next, we lined up at the edge of the sidewalk before we could keep walking. Then, we lined up in front of the cafeteria before we could enter.

It's amazing what three real meals a day can do for you. This does not exist in the real world. The apple juice in the cafeteria was always fermented. I would say, "Have you tasted this? It tastes like beer. Crazy."

We had scheduled times for daily showers, medicine distributions, and designated laundry days. Everyone woke up early, went to bed early, and had something to do every day. Depressed people thrive under strict schedules. This is another illusion that rehab offers. No bad moods went unnoticed. You almost had to try harder not to get endless support. Anywhere else looked like utter chaos compared to this.

On my second day at Children's Farm Home, the two girls in the room across the hall asked me to room with them. They had an extra bed and thought I was cool. I chose the top bunk. We ended up having what was basically a slumber party. We danced inappropriately. We laughed when our favorite staff member to flirt with caught a glimpse of us dancing inappropriately. We laughed at nothing. We forgot what had brought us there.

What had brought me there? I had no right to think my life was so awful. Haley, my new roommate, deserved to be there. Her father had raped her from ages seven to fourteen. She had his baby when she was ten. She had to pretend that her daughter was her cousin, that is when her aunt would actually let Haley see her. Her aunt's side of the family doesn't even believe she was raped.

"Wow, compared to that, I really have nothing to complain about. I mean, I've had it totally easy."

"It's not a contest, Hannah."

She told me how her brother was a Crip and she used to date a Blood. She told me about the time her boyfriend put a gun to her head and said if she didn't shoot her brother, he would shoot her. She told me about getting into fights at school. She told me about her own self-harm. She gave me cocoa butter to help with my scars. I still think of her whenever I smell it.

When she heard me tossing and turning in my bed one night, she tried to calm me down. She invited me down to her bed and went through her little key ring of multicolored cards, trying to find a skill to help me.

"What about this one? IMPROVE: Imagery, Meaning, Prayer, Relaxation, One thing in the moment, Vacation, and

Encouragement. Or ACCEPTS: Activities, Contributing, Comparisons, Emotions, Pushing away, Thoughts, and Sensations."

"I have no idea what any of this is, Haley!"

"Okay, how about Opposite to Emotion Action. You're sad, right? You have to force yourself to get active instead of withdrawing."

"How am I supposed to get active at 2 AM?"

She sat there, trying to help me. She barely knew me. We laughed, we danced, we talked. We had known each other for only two days, yet she truly cared about me. Things speed up in rehab. We were best friends.

When she went back to Newport to testify against her dad, the staff wouldn't let her stay with friends or family. She had to stay in a shelter. I was enraged. No one was allowed to hurt her. She left and asked me to take care of her fish for the four days she was gone.

I fell apart. She was the only thing keeping me going at rehab. With her there, I was the happy one in the house. I was drama-free. I readily volunteered to do chores, counseled my peers, sang "Lollipop" to all the girls. But when Haley left, I had to deal with reality.

One day when we were watching movies and having a small snack, the fire alarm went off. We lined up outside, facing the cottage. In that one second, something snapped. My "primary," the main staff member assigned to me, immediately saw the change on my face. I told him nothing was wrong. But the world had gotten darker. My primary told a joke: "Two peanuts were walking down a back alley. One was a-salted." I laughed so hard at that dumb joke, and then everything changed. I didn't laugh again for five days.

I couldn't smile. I could barely talk. I locked myself in the downstairs bathroom, not knowing what was going on in my head, not knowing what to do with myself. I volunteered to paint the basement, a least favorite activity, so I could be alone. This backfired because apparently I was popular enough to make others follow suit. I went to every meal, skipped the food line, and filled up a glass of water and drank it. I didn't consume any food for four days. At every possible moment, I was back in bed.

Even though I was there for depression and suicide, the staff had never seen me like this. My primary, usually gruff and removed, whom I loved to tease to try to soften him up, suddenly got very worried. He tried to get me to talk, to do things, to trick me into smiling. The psychiatrist switched me from time-released to regular Wellbutrin. But it was my counselor who was effectively abrupt about getting me well.

John, my counselor, was the type of mentor you see in movies. He was like Robin Williams in *Dead Poets Society*, teaching me amazing things about myself—a genius, possibly totally crazy himself. He did things like challenge me to spell difficult words at the beginning of every session to make me feel good, tell me stories of his wild childhood, and tell me to scream at him. He said, "You know what we do here if you cut yourself? We give you a Band-Aid." And, "You shouldn't kill yourself. You know why? Because then I don't get to treat you."

He analyzed me. It was astounding. He once said, "I think the reason you have such low self-esteem is because when you were young, too young to have object permanence, your mother wasn't there because she was in and out of the psych ward and your father was too depressed to be emotionally present and your sisters were young and worried about taking care of themselves. Your family was basically gone and you had no way of knowing if they were ever coming back. You couldn't blame it on your parents because at that age, your parents are God, they can do no wrong. You had to blame their absence on yourself. That way you had control over getting them back, all you had to do was be good. But you couldn't be good, because if you were good and they were still gone, that would mean that they were wrong, which is impossible. So you were always bad. And you always had to tell yourself that you were a bad person. You're still doing that today."

At the end of the four days of near-catatonic depression in Haley's absence, I finally had a session with John.

"So, what's been going on, Hannah?"

"I haven't been eating."

"I know. You know what you should do? Go to dinner and eat a quarter of everything on your tray. If you get sixteen peas, eat four. Got it?"

"Okay. I'll try it."

Just like that. No reason for why I wasn't eating was needed to get me eating again. Starvation was the problem at hand. I was up to full meals by the next day, and just taking care of myself physically in and of itself made me feel better. And then Haley was back.

She said that the necklace I gave her helped her out. I had been making jewelry by knotting rainbow yarn. She wore hers on the stand. She said her father got only seven years because she had tried to change her story at one point. I held back my anger and told her that she was going to be in a totally different place when she was twenty-one, and for a solid seven years, her dad would be raped in the ass in prison. She laughed.

After that, I was pretty happy. I worked on my issues in therapy, but mostly I was having fun and helping others. We watched old movies and gave each other facials. We joked and sang and flirted with the staff. We went swimming, horseback riding, played foosball, painted the basement, did chores, played basketball and board games, and went on little trips. We volunteered by cleaning up a park, went shopping a few times, hiked, and took a trip up to Portland for the Italian Festival. We sang the whole way there and back. The Italian Festival was just food, so we went shopping at Pioneer Place, which was brand-new to most everyone but me. I wrote an article about it for the newsletter. I got my face painted and handed out snow cones at the end-of-summer fair. I was having a blast and did a little work on myself.

When I had to leave, it felt way too soon. The psychiatrist thought he could get me a few more days, and when he told me he couldn't, I burst out crying. I was happy in this controlled environment, and even he agreed I wasn't ready to apply it at home. He would've liked more time, but the insurance wouldn't allow it. Staff and patients wrote things in my good-bye book, often about how much I had helped them or how much the kids looked up to me. One of the girls, who had arrived there from juvie and disrupted the whole house, gave me a hug. She didn't get along with anyone and refused to comply with any rules. Her first day, she kept every staff member in the living room, attending to her tantrum about not having any clothes. I offered her mine. When I left, she said I was the one person there who was cool. Friends wrote down inside jokes in my book and did their best to give me contact information, but it was hard because they were mostly foster kids. On my last day, everyone sat in a circle and said nice things about me. I never wanted to leave.

The drive home was awkward. I didn't want my family. I didn't want to go home. I didn't want to be anywhere but at the Children's Farm Home with a support system and schedule and constant care and help. We stopped at a music store and I walked around. A darkness hit me. I had never felt so lost and haven't since. I stood there, sure that the darkness would swallow me whole. That grief didn't leave me for a while. I never again had that kind of care and structure. I was never able to re-create the comfort I felt there because the world is a scary place. Now, although I know how to cope with the bad and enjoy the good, it never stops being scary. I'm just okay with being scared.

Sustenance

"PUT IT DOWN. THROW IT AWAY. You are gigantic; you are morbidly obese. You weighed two hundred seven pounds a few months ago, and you still have a long way to go. You don't deserve food."

"Come on, don't be insane. You're a little overweight and you're not going to lose all those pounds in one long fast. All of this abstaining is only making your metabolism worse. It's only a salad, and you haven't eaten in, what, three days? You need to eat."

"Yeah, that would be a great point if you were skinny. That isn't even lite dressing. And croutons? Are you kidding me? Do you want to become Jabba the Hut? Don't you want anyone to love you ever again?"

This is the inner dialogue that goes on in my head, the argument between the little angel and devil hovering over my shoulders whenever I sit down to eat. The only problem is, I don't know which one is which. Things got really bad when I was dropping out of school and I had nothing else to do but obsess over food. That habit really hasn't gone away.

Let me back up. My obsession didn't come out of nowhere. It was precipitated by years of confusion about food.

When I was young, I was dangerously thin. I would eat only a few things, namely toast and ketchup, cold hot dogs, and Kraft Macaroni & Cheese. This could have been one of my reactions to my parents' divorce, but more likely, I was just a really picky kid. As I grew older, I began to eat a few more things, but most things I refused. If my parents could convince me to try something, everyone at the table had to look away while I ate it. I felt paranoid that people were staring at me at the dinner table.

The first time I remember feeling fat was in the fifth grade. I doubt I had gained more than a few pounds, but society's allowance for baby fat was wearing thin. My grandmother pulled me aside and told me to watch my weight. My mother's anorexia and my stepmom's constant dieting made me even more confused about food's role in my life. Carol tried to help me eat healthier. I started to hide junk food in my room. Eating became my dirty little secret.

Middle school started and cliques formed, boys and girls dated, and our bodies were on display as adolescence transformed us. Puberty made me curvy. With my period came boobs, butt, and a layer of fat all around. Still, I couldn't have been more than 140 pounds and a size ten. It would have been fine if I'd had an ounce of self-esteem; however, this was also the time when my severe depression emerged. Kids can be cruel and I was humiliated every day in gym class, in those awful uniform shorts, when I failed to run a mile in under ten minutes or do sit-ups without someone holding my feet. My low confidence hit bottom.

I started ninth grade two days out of rehab. I had to learn the hard way how important those three balanced meals a day and regular exercise were when I gained back the ten pounds I had lost while at the Children's Farm Home. Still, in a size twelve I managed to attract my first boyfriend. I tried not to compare myself to my tall, thin best friend and chose to be cherished by Ty.

Ty truly loved me. I didn't know that until later. But with good grades, speech and debate success, a long-awaited group of true friends, and Ty, I was happy. I wasn't even thinking about food. I knew that he appreciated my body, not only because of his words, but because of his hands. He even respected my body. We never did anything too serious physically, and I didn't know how important this was to me until Frank came along.

In the spring of ninth grade, when all the enchantment of life anew fell away, I fell into the same familiar depression. My eating showed this. Nicole and I were practically bragging to each other about how many days we could go without food when we were upset. For me, starving myself was just punishment when I was unhappy, but Nicole was so skinny already, I didn't realize how dangerous it was to allow her to do this. But it wasn't just my eating that suffered. I relapsed with cutting, I broke up with Ty, I tried to kill myself, and soon after, I met Frank.

Frank used to be obese and had lost a lot of weight. This made his emotional control over me extend to food. He would scold me for drinking soda or reprimand me for eating chips. On one of our late-night excursions, we went to IHOP. I was craving a sundae. He, of course, disapproved, so I ordered a salad instead. When I went to the hospital to visit a close friend who had tried to kill himself, I bought a candy bar from the gift shop to cheer myself up. When I called Frank to pick me up, he lectured me for it. Near the end of our relationship, I was afraid to eat anything.

By the time I found Matthew during my junior year, I couldn't let him near my body. I loved him. I would have given him my virginity if I hadn't hated my body so much. He thought I was beautiful. I was unable to believe him. When he broke my heart, I really lost it. I weighed in at two hundred seven pounds. I never thought I would ever have to slide the weight on that ancient scale over to the two hundred mark and then count up from there. I was appalled. I didn't recognize my body. All of my emotional eating had finally caught up with me.

When I hit rock bottom, I took my redemption too far. I stopped eating.

For a couple of months, anyway, I was the world's best fat anorexic. Our house has two kitchens because it was meant for two families. My siblings had all grown up and moved out, so the downstairs kitchen was all mine. By looking at it, no one would be able to tell it was functional. All of the food had run out. The refrigerator was bare. I didn't see the need in restocking it because I wasn't going to need the food. There were a lot of zero-calorie mixed drinks and a few choice items for me to chew and spit out. That is if I wasn't in the mood for throwing up.

I had a system. I could eat little-to-no calories on the weekdays, then pig out on the weekends. This was because I had no privacy at my mom's apartment, which is where I spent my weekends. But then, pig-outs were not allowed. So, I started eating healthy food and skipping meals at my mom's. Then I stopped going to her house completely. That way I could barely eat for twelve days straight. That was my record, anyway. If any exceptions had to be made, they could easily be vomited into the kitchen sink. Of course, I couldn't vomit if I had just taken my weight-loss supplements.

I knew it was not enough to just stop eating. I needed to do more than cut out calories—I had to burn them. I power-walked around the neighborhood for up to an hour. I sprinted in the backyard as long as I could take it. I did cardio tapes until I passed out. I started playing the numbers game, too. I told myself I didn't have an eating disorder like the girl who'd told me about her number-eleven game. I would start eating healthy again when I was happy with my progress or when I was in a position to buy my own food. This was just temporary. Still, I wasn't about to take any chances where superstitions were concerned. I held my body in a push-up position, resting on my forearms, for one minute eleven seconds. I jogged up and down the balcony steps twenty-two times. Twenty-two sit-ups, thirty-three jumping jacks, twenty-two toe touches, twenty-two pelvic thrusts, eighty-eight elbow-to-knees, ninety-nine crunches.

When I felt too weak to stand, I could tell myself to stop being insane, to eat something because it wouldn't be the end of the world. I could allow myself to leave some of the salad unpurged. I could allow myself to do a slightly modified exercise routine. I told myself I had lost only twenty pounds, not nearly enough to be considered a problem. Maybe if I was starving myself and I was skinny, *then* it would be a disorder. *Then* it would be dangerous. *Then* I could eat a little something. But I knew that when I walked down the street, people thought, "Why doesn't she just stop eating?" I knew that I was the only person alive who didn't deserve food. When big people lose weight, they get congratulated for being healthy. No one would assume that a fat person losing weight was emotionally unhealthy. No one would consider that eating restrictions were a response to stress like they might if a thin person were to do the same thing. No one would nay-say if they were sick of looking at your fat face.

I went to New York for a week and allowed myself to stray. I tried a chickpea burger. I ate authentic New York–style pizza. I had espresso and gelato at the Museum of Modern Art. I devoured a south Indian feast of masala dosa, pani puri, iddly, sambar, and coconut chutney. It renewed my faith that life could be happy and exciting. Food was a big part of my joy. I laughed at how I thought I could be content by removing food from my life.

When I got home and realized I had gained back ten of the twenty pounds I had lost, I did not fret. I decided to look at weight loss differently. I knew I couldn't lose all this weight quickly, so I had to approach it logically. I had to

First Boyfriends

I ARRIVED AS A NINTH GRADER at Evergreen High School two days out of rehab. I didn't have much time to finish the summer reading, which turned out to be a good thing, seeing as *Member of the Wedding* is the worst book ever and should be read as quickly as possible. I took choir and German and tried to join way too many clubs. I needed a whole new set of friends, and I got it.

I started hanging out with a new group of kids, half guys, half girls. We were like Archie and his gang, complete with a boy named Moose. Out of all of my new friends, Nicole, whom I'd known from eighth grade choir and health, became my new best friend.

Our group would hang out in the Junior Hall, sitting on

the floor in a circle or running around. We would draw on one another with Sharpies. We would leave campus, sometimes skipping fourth period as well, driving to get food. Nicole and I weren't allowed to leave campus at all, since we were the only freshman of the bunch, but we liked acting just as cool as the upperclassmen. We would go off into the woods to smoke, looking to see if the security guard coming toward us was the cool one. If not, we scattered. I haven't had that much fun since.

When Nicole and I started going out with some of the guys from the group, things got messy. Nicole started dating Tannon, then broke up with him to date Rich. I started flirting with Ty. On the last day before Christmas break, Nicole, Rich, Ty, and I hung out in the hallways, running around, being physically flirtatious. I used Rich's phone to call home and tell my dad I'd be late. Ty stealthily got my number off Rich's cell and called me the next day. I liked him too much to consider this as stalker behavior. He made me absolutely giddy. My stepmom called me a smitten kitten—I couldn't stop smiling. My mom's only phone has a chord and it was in the living room. I talked to Ty for impolite amounts of time while stuck in my mom's apartment with my sister.

By the time New Year's Eve came, Nicole and Rich were officially together, and Ty and I were on the verge of going out. I had the New Year's Eve party at my place, and as soon as Ty came into the house, he sat next to me and whispered, "Wanna go out with me?" Of course I said yes.

I received my first kiss that night, but it wasn't at midnight. I was standing in the dining room and he was standing behind me. When I turned to look at him, he suddenly leaned in and kissed me. It was surprisingly smooth for a first kiss, and it felt magical. I ran to my group of girlfriends, told them about it, and we squealed. They then told him, "If you hurt her, we will beat you with bendy straws." Later that night when he brushed past my freshly pierced ear and I said, "Ow!" all of my friends picked up bendy straws and began beating him with them. We pretty much spent the rest of the night making out.

Unfortunately, things weren't off to as great a start between Nicole and Rich. Rich refused to show Nicole any attention that night so as not to make Katie, our friend who had a crush on him, jealous. At one point, I found Nicole in my room and had to coax her back to the party. It ended with us all crammed in the guest room watching *The Rocky Horror Picture Show*. Ty was cuddling me, but Rich was still being distant with Nicole. It wouldn't be the first time he would play mind games with her.

Since I'd never had a boyfriend before, I had no idea how my new relationship would go into effect once winter break was over. The first day back at school, I was walking over to the student store for some chai when someone grabbed my waist. I turned around and was shocked to see Ty. He kissed me and we walked together, holding hands, between almost every class. Since he had much more dating experience, I let him take the lead. It took me quite a while to realize that I actually hated PDA (Public Display of Affection) and the ridicule we got for making out in public.

Nicole and Rich were all over each other, too. She and I used to compete to see how far we went with our respective boy toys. At first we were even, but since Ty was Catholic, our activity didn't go past necking and under-the-bra groping. Nicole beat me until it wasn't even a competition anymore. But as their sexuality escalated, so did their arguing.

She would tell me every time he acted like a dumbass. Even though he used to be sweet all the time, he started showing a different side of himself—a side that didn't like to be wrong. On one of their late-night talks (of which they had many because he demanded they talk every day), Nicole mentioned that she heard a train. He insisted there was no way she'd heard a train, that there were no railroads within earshot of her house. So she went online and found there was a railroad only a few miles from her house, definitely within earshot. When she told Rich, he went ballistic. "You went behind my back just to prove me wrong? How dare you not believe me?!"

Ty and I didn't argue—we just teased each other. Actually, everyone teased Ty. They made fun of him for being a Catholic redhead. At first, it didn't get to me. I thought he was cute and that was all that mattered. I went to church with him and his family, and he made me French toast afterward. I went to his youth group dance and surprised him when I knew the prayer we said before dinner.

On Valentine's Day, he gave me a rose and wrote me a poem. He was always telling me how beautiful and smart I was. I felt absolutely cherished. I told him about the

Children's Farm Home and why I had been there. He told me about the time he pressed charges against his father for beating him. We accepted each other.

Nicole and Rich continued to fight, though. Even though they had good times, they knew how to press each other's buttons. Both Ty and Rich had their anger problems, but at least Ty had never taken them out on me. Rich would get so angry that he would kick holes in the door, punch holes in the wall, throw and break CDs. He would belittle and demean Nicole when his life was stressful, and she would hold it in until it was time for a big blowout. Then he would not only yell at her for the issue at hand but also for bottling up her emotions. She said she wouldn't have to if he didn't get so mad every time she questioned him. He never hit her, but one time he got so angry he punched the shelf above his bed, knocking over a heavy glass, which fell on Nicole's face. Another time they were fighting and he made a motion with his arm. He got mad at her for flinching as if he would hit her. The fights were bad, but they were infrequent enough that I wasn't too alarmed yet. Since I was new to dating, I didn't know what was going too far in a relationship.

I didn't know that Rich was emotionally abusing Nicole.

At the time, I was actually more alarmed by Ty's anger. Even though he never hurt me, he twisted Nicole's arm once in a play-fight and told me later that he scared himself because he wanted to keep twisting. After his dad beat him up, he got into a slap-fight in the hallway. It was supposed to be just for fun, but he ended up getting hurt when he wouldn't quit. When a guy in my math class started calling me names, Ty was intent on defending me. He got into a physical confrontation with the offender. He was often ready to explode. And one day he did.

It was stupid. I was wearing Ty's Nike swoosh sweatshirt. A stoner in my class said, "Hey, did you know that if you switch the *sw* with a *d* you get douche?"

From then on he called me douche lady. It wasn't very creative and I wasn't offended, but Ty was furious. Apparently they made fun of the same thing when he wore that hoodie his freshman year.

"When they insult me, it's okay, but when they go after my girlfriend . . ."

"Violence doesn't solve anything. Please don't do anything, not over something this dumb," I told him.

He said he wouldn't. Then he did. I had never witnessed a fistfight before. It was awful. I started crying in Nicole's arms when it started. I didn't see the rest. I didn't want to. I just went into the bathroom.

I heard it was a fair fight before it was broken up, but some said Ty lost. He said that the other guy had a fist pack. I didn't care either way. Ty got suspended from school and walked straight to the hotel where his dad worked. Apparently his dad's reaction fell somewhere in between ambivalence and pride. It was clear to me where Ty got the idea that violence was acceptable. Still, when he called me, he expected me to yell at him. I didn't. I just asked him if he got what he wanted. I told him that it hurt me, not just that he fought, but that he broke his promise to me that he wouldn't fight. He thought I was breaking up with him. I wasn't. I couldn't hold his faulty upbringing or his need to defend me against him. I just hoped his black eye was punishment enough.

On our three-month anniversary, I saw someone from the school floral shop delivering yellow balloons. I said, "Ooh! Yellow!"

"Are you Hannah?" he said.

"Uh, yeah?"

"These are for you."

The card had the words I LOVE YOU printed on it, and Ty had written "Three months today. Have a good spring break. Ty." I told myself he couldn't possibly be telling me that he loved me, not this way.

It was spring break right after our three-month anniversary, and I went away with Katie and her mom to the beach for a week. I didn't call Ty once. Katie and I shopped and flirted with guys to get free stuff. We wore skimpy clothes and flirted with more guys. Of course, they were more interested in Katie, with her giant breasts and obvious experience, but I was happy to get some of the attention. I had fun and started to think I was bored with Ty. When I got back from the beach, nothing felt the same. For me, anyway.

Ty's birthday was the day after I got back. I realized how little I cared about him anymore by how hard it was for me to find him a present. I got him a cheesy card. Then I got him a funny book and ended up keeping it, because I remembered his joking about how lame it was to get books as presents. So I got him a gift card to a music store instead. I said it was because I was trying to expand his music knowledge, but we both knew that gift cards were impersonal.

I broke up with him a few days later. I told him I was getting more depressed and needed to change some things. I wanted to have my birthday without him, which was a week after his. It turned out that he had already gotten me a birthday present—a Sarah McLachlan CD, because he knew she was my favorite at the time, and a laser pointer, because we had a running joke about distracting cats with them. I felt guilty. My birthday party was girls only and it was good for recuperation, but I still despised myself.

Less than a month later, I attempted suicide. I realized in retrospect that I hadn't been bored with Ty when I broke up with him. I was bored with life.

When I got back from the hospital following my suicide attempt, Ty ran up to me and hugged me. But things would never be the same. He found out I was dating a twenty-year-old and got pissed. We argued about his joining the military. My sister lectured him when I dressed in drag for a week as a social experiment and he called me a freak. We fought more than we ever did when we were together. Maybe it's because he loved me. He walked to my house one afternoon to tell me so, and to tell me that his love for me was unconditional whether we were together or not. I felt bad that I couldn't tell him I loved him, too.

* * *

By the time we got to tenth grade, I was still single, but Nicole and Rich were still going strong. In fact, Nicole decided she was going to give her virginity to Rich on his graduation day that spring. Then they decided to move that up to prom night, then to Valentine's Day, then to New Year's Eve, which would be their one-year anniversary.

I knew how much of her life Rich already controlled, and I was worried that he was coercing her to move up the date. But when I tried to convince her to stick to the original plan, she got mad at me for not minding my own business. I was left sobbing in my room, reminded of how Frank had used his influence and power over me to speed things up. I couldn't make Nicole listen to me, but it was hard to watch her go through the same thing I had. In the end, Nicole ended up having sex with Rich on New Year's, after a nice dinner, surrounded by candles, and listening to the Eagles. Today she says she doesn't regret the way she lost her virginity, just whom she gave it to.

Over the next few months, I continued to hear stories, almost daily, about horrible things Rich had done. He would cut her off when she talked about something important to her and refuse to show her any affection in public, almost as if he were embarrassed to be seen with her. When she told him that she felt fat, he would say, "Go work out, then." He offered to buy her breast implants. The first time he broke up with her, she didn't eat for more than a week.

As Nicole's best friend, I couldn't just stand by and watch. Rich would disrespect her, use her, make her feel terrible about herself, and she would keep going back. But every time I tried to get involved and protect her, she wouldn't listen to me, or worse, she would get mad at me. The whole thing was starting to affect me more than I knew, and I would call my therapist, sobbing. I was exhausted from worrying about Nicole and trying to get her away from Rich. Finally, my friend and I gave her an ultimatum: leave him or lose us as friends. I wanted to show her how serious we were and what she was losing, but also I couldn't bear to witness this anymore. She chose Rich.

Nicole and I didn't speak for a year and a half. Not in person anyway. Eventually, we made up over MySpace and made small talk every once in a while. But she and Rich were still doing their destructive thing. He would yell at her, emotionally abuse her, and she would let him.

Finally, she broke up with him once and for all. She went to California for her great-grandmother's funeral. It was a joyous experience to be at a family reunion of sorts after being so isolated. She texted Rich, "We need to talk."

"Is it a good thing or a bad thing?" he asked.

"Bad thing."

"Now?" he responded.

"No, I'm at the mall."

On the phone later, she broke it off with him.

"Don't do this while you're in California," he said.

"No, I'm going to do this while I have the nerve."

"We can work on it. I love you."

"No we can't. I don't have those feelings anymore."

"You know you're never gonna find anyone else who's gonna put up with your shit like I have!"

"I have to go to dinner."

She says that this breakup actually stuck because she wasn't mad . . . she was just done.

Soon after she and Rich broke up for good, I demanded that Nicole and I finally get together. I knew if we didn't before she left for college in California, we would never see each other again.

We met at her mom's office at Portland State University. We got salads at a cafe and then took the bus to a disappointing apron exhibit. We went to the $6 store, the nickel arcade, and a pizza parlor that was having a Balkan night, where we joined in with the Balkan dancers. We went to Voodoo Doughnuts and to the eighteen-and-over strip club. We ended up with chili cheese fries at the Roxy and called a cab to take us back to my grandparents' house.

The next morning I told my mom, "We haven't seen each other in a year and a half and there were zero awkward silences! We picked up just where we left off!"

Though I did what I could at the time, I still regret not

being there when Nicole went through the worst parts of her relationship with Rich. Today, she's with Tony, who seems to be the love of her life. Tony and I went with her as she pawned the ring that Rich gave her. She has nothing left of Rich besides a cautionary tale for her little sister.

Second Overdose

I HAD STOPPED TAKING MY WELLBUTRIN. When I cleaned my room, I found forty-five of them. I put them all in a pile and took each one. I regretted it a little. Over the phone, my friend begged me to make myself throw up, but I couldn't. I figured I would just sleep it off, but it had the opposite effect. Later that night, it kicked in and I started hallucinating. I saw spiders crawling all over my room, bats flying, rats in the corners. I had to get out of my bedroom, but I didn't want to wake my parents. I looked out the window of my second floor bedroom and watched as my front lawn bounced and settled just under my sill. I climbed out and fell, shrieking on impact as I broke my foot. It felt important enough to me at the time not to worry my parents that I walked the nearly two miles to Nicole's house in the middle of the night. I was screaming and crying at the pain in every step. I limped while I hallucinated whole people in the dark. I ended up in front of a bar, and a strange man offered to help.

"Yes, can you please just give me a ride to my friend's house?"

"Well, I rode here with someone else, but are you sure I can't call 9-1-1 for you?"

"No, I just need to walk to my friend's house!"

I was banging on my friend's window and screaming when her mother came and took me inside.

"I'm seeing spiders and people and rats and they won't go away and my foot hurts so bad because I jumped out my window and I don't know what's going on and I walked here and I'm so scared!"

"Hannah, calm down. Did you take something?"

"Yeah, I took a bunch of my antidepressants."

She iced my foot and called my parents. Nicole came out of her room in a daze. She had no idea what was going on, but she gave me a stuffed Pooh Bear and waited with me.

My parents took me to the ER, where the doctors, this

time mistakenly, again said it was too late to pump my stomach. I saw colorful darts in the ceiling and insisted that my stepmother double-check that they weren't actually there. I had to ask if every other word was, in fact, a real word. The spiders still had not disappeared. I was unable to control my urination. I was on my period and they gave me a pad and some strange netting underwear so they could still fit in the catheter. I barely knew where, or who, I was.

In the bathroom, still clumsy on my foot brace, I slipped and blacked out, knocking over a cart of toilet paper. I started seizing and vomiting chunks of the pills. It went on like this, a dozen doctors and nurses working on me, holding me down, then tipping me on my side when one doctor yelled, "Over!" and I had to vomit again. My parents watched the whole thing. I don't know how long it took to get stabilized and wake up, but when I did, I convinced everyone that I could be released. I told them it was an accident, I'd be fine in outpatient—I have to go to school. But really, it was because I knew my parents couldn't afford it if I were admitted to rehab.

Nicole and her mother came to visit. We slowly walked down the hall and laughed hysterically. It was painfully obvious that I was faking it. She brought me several notes that she had written in class, chock full of silly inside jokes.

They let me go home, only to be greeted by every friend, family member, and stranger who wanted to know why I was in a foot brace and a neck brace. My ex-boyfriend rushed to hug me. My choir teacher wouldn't let me take my final until I told him what happened, and he wouldn't take "attacked by Coca-Cola polar bears at the zoo because I was drinking Pepsi" for an answer. My friend Jackie stuck to that story until she was kicked out of choir, but I caved when I was alone in my choir teacher's office. He awkwardly told me, "Well, you should take your medication from now on," and I proceeded to awkwardly fail that test.

My parents had to change my neck brace pads, slowly so as not to move my neck. When we went to the hospital a few weeks later to get the neck brace off, I decided to keep it. The following Halloween, along with a cocktail dress and some makeup for blood and bruises, I used the neck brace to go as A Classy Prostitute Whose John Roughed Her Up. I had gotten my sense of humor back. Sick as it was, I could laugh again. I still keep the neck brace as a reminder.

The Trial

I AM HYPERAWARE OF MYSELF on the ride to the Child Abuse Intervention Center. Dad is driving me to my deposition. Does my makeup make me look like jailbait? Do my breasts look big enough that no man should be held responsible for his advances? Is my jacket overcompensation for routine sluttiness? The spiel of self-deprecation went off and sent my schema flying. Am I supposed to be young and naïve or mature and eloquent? The sweet victim or the reliable witness? I don't expect the atmosphere to be jovial, but that'll be the deciding factor of whether or not to show my corruption.

I am not ready to be deposed. The trial had been set months in advance, so my mind was fixed on it never coming.

It was a far-off, abstract concept that would always be weeks away. It would never be tomorrow or today or right now, except that it is today and it is right now and I am on the car ride there. It's time for meditation. The strangest things come to your mind when it is clear.

"How committed are you to staying alive, Hannah?" I hear my therapist's voice in my head. I didn't know how to answer.

* * *

The lawyer's name was Beau. That made the whole thing ten times worse. He introduced himself not as Mr. Johnston but as Beau, then flashed a grin. I almost expected him to wink and offer to buy me a drink. He told me my whole medical history in question form. *His* version of the story, that is. That's exactly what it was. The defense lawyer of the man charged with raping me knew more about me than my own attorney did. Around and around the table they ask me if I was feeling vengeful or if my therapist told me to say this or that. They dragged the rudest and crudest aspects of my life out onto the table. No more grins were being flashed, I can assure you.

"Have you ever hallucinated?"

I requested a break. A little reassurance from my advocate in the adjacent room, a few deep breaths in the bathroom, and it was back to the firing squad, visibly drained.

"I really don't think these questions are relevant to this case," I said.

"Well, it really doesn't matter what you think. Answer the question. Have you ever hallucinated?" Slap in the face.

Maybe, objectively, this was their last resort. People laughed and told me to try not to feel too bad for the losing team. But I never thought every detail of my past would be held against me, against my character and credibility, against my integrity.

"I'm sure we're all sensitive to the allegations being made," Beau said.

Sensitive is not how I would describe how I was being treated.

The defense ultimately settled for probation and work crew after almost three years of torturous delays. Three years of avoiding our town mall where my rapist worked, of panicking when I saw a car similar to his, of crying every few months when my rape advocate called to say the trial had been postponed again.

He pled guilty to what he was charged with, as long as they called it Communication with a Minor with Immoral Purposes instead of Rape of a Child. Even after he had settled, after he had gotten what he wanted, the attorney felt the need to publicly discredit me. He told the judge that I was a crazy, suicidal, pill-popping cutter. I was only informed of the Health Information Privacy Act in front of the courthouse after it was all over, when the prosecutor told me I had the right to not answer questions about my psychiatric history. So very helpful.

My English teacher was the prosecutor's brother and the spitting image of him. I stopped going to that class. I stopped going to all my classes. I lost my friends.

How did it come to this?

* * *

I never want to feel this again. The hard extremities of his body pushed inside me and when it didn't hurt, it was just disgusting. *How did I get here? I am drunk, that's for sure. Half a bottle of vodka can do that to you. I asked for this. I could take my liquor better than he could. I'm letting him drive me home drunk tonight. Why are the rocks on this beach not sand?*

"What are you thinking?" he asked.

"I was thinking that that was the most predictable cliché you could have ever fulfilled." My sarcastic tone should have told him to back off. *On the beach. How trite. How fucking romantic. I told him not to let me do anything I wouldn't do sober.*

"You're so articulate with your words."

"What else would I be articulate with?" He was such a child. He was twenty.

"You know what I mean. Shit, I am drunk." He hadn't had as much to drink as I had.

"So am I."

"I know. I could tell that when you were rolling down the hill."

Was that a metaphor? My downfall leading to this point? Or maybe to the point I reached when he was at his first hearing and I was in a bathtub full of my own blood, screaming 9-1-1.

"I would have done that even if I was sober." I was fifteen. Fifteen and two months, if you want to be specific. I was young and not so jaded that I couldn't do things like roll down hills for fun.

How did we get here? We had climbed over the seawall behind Who Song and Larry's Mexican restaurant. I wouldn't be able to drive past this place again without a hand to squeeze. *This is private property. My eye shadow is smeared. He doesn't like it when I wear makeup. He rubs it off. He says what I'm wearing is weird. I feel nauseous.*

"I feel nauseous."

He sighed and let his head hit the pebbles. "Okay, let's go back up."

Why did I give him my sexuality when things were going sour? How long have we been dating? Three weeks? Oh, I am so drunk. Where did the rest of this conversation go?

I had started "doing things" with him when we ran out of things to talk about, when everything I said was immature. *But, then, why would a twenty-year-old date a fifteen-year-old unless she was especially mature?* It wasn't long before I was stirring my drinks with my sunglasses; not instinctually, but to attract his attention with the alluring quirks that reeled him in at the beginning.

I had been friends with his ex-girlfriend, Marie, who was two years older than me. My friend Briana and I had met her in our ninth-grade German class, and we were hanging out at her house one day after school, wondering who we could get to drive us to Taco Bell. Marie called Frank. We listened to *Abbey Road* on the way to Value Village, where we tried on ridiculous outfits. We went home and watched *Waking Life*. I fell asleep on him.

We texted and talked on MySpace. It didn't faze me that he was so much older because I thought I was very mature. We ran into each other at Fort Vancouver on the Fourth of July and I rested on him as we watched the fireworks show.

When the fireworks ended, he invited me to see the midnight showing of *Pirates of the Caribbean 2* with him. I was supposed to get a ride home from my friend's mom afterward, but I didn't care. I was young and feeling adventurous, so I had Frank drive me instead, telling myself there was no way I could find my friend's mom in this crowd, anyway. Then I told Frank not to drive me home, to drive anywhere. We drove and talked and got chai at the Roxy.

We were out all night and I came home in the morning to

screaming parents and a cop. They insisted that he kidnapped me. They assumed that we were dating, probably that we had sex. They refused to believe that I didn't even know his last name. They wanted him arrested. I was sobbing. It was all very dramatic.

Despite the drama of that first night, our relationship was naively magical at the beginning. It was blazing lights, dark roads, and life stories. The world's spotlights were on us and we felt beautiful. The dialogue was scripted and forgettable. The only times he touched me were to protect and comfort, much as a brother would do. We started dating after that night, while I was grounded, and I sneaked out to see him. Our wild romance should have ended when it started. I asked for what I got by continuing it. I only violated myself.

No, that's not true. He took advantage. And that fateful night on the beach wasn't the first time, either. Just a week before he did something worth three to five years, he took advantage of me when I was more vulnerable than I ever could have been while drunk.

It was the hottest night of the year. I was in a thin tank top and a miniskirt, and the heat was still unbearable. I spent my insomnia with him. Like every Saturday night, my mom's meds lullabied her to sleep like clockwork and I summoned my Romeo and fled the castle.

He stood there offering a genuine smile. I ran to him like he himself was the getaway car. A couple of hours passed after we ditched his car at the Reed campus. We walked through the industrial areas and found a park. There he made me a promise. Somehow I lost all my self-respect in that moment . . . something in my mind snapped. I later realized I'd had a panic attack, wherein delusions were reasonable. I guess my psyche thought imagined monsters were better than the man beside me, offering friendly molestation.

We were trying to find the car. It was Portland—my neighborhood, not his. My childhood, his strange land. I was definitely leading. It was just so hot and dark, it felt new to me, threatening. The bushes we walked by intimidated me. My hands were so tight, just like the fists of a revolutionary, fists ready to fight those damn bushes. Knuckles against knuckles were rubbing and peeling back skin. I kept looking back over my shoulder with shifty, suspicious eyes. I knew we were being followed, for I could hear that third party and feel its presence on my back. Then, all these shapes of creatures with sparks for eyes emerged from the dark. I was breathing heavily, giving myself a headache, getting weak. I couldn't speak.

It went on like this, with him stopping every once in a while so that I wouldn't faint. He kept asking me what I heard, what I saw. He couldn't understand that what I heard didn't make sense and that the creatures I saw were indescribable. I couldn't let him touch me. We were lost. He said, "Just kiss me; it'll make things better, I promise." He spoke in the softest voice, and he stood there so beautiful, but I couldn't look him in the eye and I certainly couldn't let him kiss me. I cringed from his arms and hugged myself instead.

This is mine, not his. These angles of my hometown aren't visible to him. These angles of my mind, my break from sanity, it is mine. He can't see it. He doesn't remember this field from the eyes of a three-year-old, and he really can't feel the panic in my chest. I need to curl up right here. I need to fold myself over until I'm small and compact. Can he not see the bats hanging from the ceiling? I can't handle this. I can't handle this. I can't . . . it's so hot. Whatever happens to me tonight will be because of my skirt. My skin is tingling . . . I wish he'd just scratch me out.

I wish I didn't hate him for doing what he did. He was molested as a boy, and I made every wrong decision I could have made. It is just that that night he executed his promise and came inside me when I couldn't tell what was real. This feeling of hate, it is mine. It will burn in my chest where that panic used to be and never be wasted on him again.

* * *

"Have you ever hallucinated?"

"Yes, Beau, I have. When I took an overdose of my antidepressants a few months before I met your client, I hallucinated. And that night he knew perfectly well what a vulnerable state I was in."

Dig your holes. Go on, do it. I've dug mine. This is me, climbing back out. This is mine to make right again.

First Love

HE NOTICED ME BEFORE I NOTICED HIM, but I approached him before he approached me.

I walked right up to him between rounds at the speech and debate tournament and said, "You have the most beautiful smile!"

This type of thing isn't uncharacteristic of me. I'm very outgoing yet easily embarrassed. I have loads of confidence despite dangerously low self-esteem. I didn't know Matthew and I didn't necessarily want to befriend or date him. Like I said, I hadn't really noticed him—I just thought he deserved to know that he had a beautiful smile.

The tournament took place during my junior year. If we had met during a freshman year speech and debate tournament, he probably would've found me crying. I despised debate, with its professionally clad students meeting at different high schools to fight one another for awards. While I did love giving planned speeches and performances, unfortunately Ms. Bray had shanghaied me into parliamentary debate. And though I've always been fiercely stubborn, the more passionate I get, the less I am able to articulate my argument. Not to mention, I knew close to nothing about what was going on in the world compared to these kids.

As a freshman, I got pummeled at the big tournament. A debate duo from Ridgefield massacred Briana and me. Ridgefield kids were bred and raised to be master debaters, and Evergreen kids were the rejects. Our E-green spirit was that of slacking off and body modification. You could tell our best debaters by how many piercings were in their heads. I fit right in. I just didn't have the skills to match yet. I was devastated. There was a lot of downtime between rounds for me to mope. By the end of the year, I was voted Least Likely to Ever Debate Again.

Despite my utter failure in the world of debate, I found my niche in speech. Ms. Bray practically put my entire interpretive reading piece together, but I interpreted the reading. The theme my freshman year was Womanhood. The pieces were from *The House on Mango Street*, *In the Land of Women*, and *Phenomenal Woman*. My introduction started with a real attention grabber—Mike Meyer's beat poem from *So I Married an Axe Murderer*. "Woman. *W*o-man. Woooooooooooooah-*man*! She was a thief. You got to belief. She stole my heart and my cat." I made a name for myself with that speech. I also made quite a few points.

My sophomore year was definitely more productive, and more rewarding. My interpretive reading was about obsession, with selections from *You Remind Me of You*, *Lolita*, and *Rules of Attraction*. Judges either emphatically loved it or told me it was inappropriate. However, what was really memorable was the way I stood up and suddenly whispered the cheesy opening line: "Obsession: more than just Calvin Klein's eau de parfume."

I also had a dramatic interpretation—a very cut-down version of *I Am My Own Wife*. The piece was about Charlotte von Mahlsdorf, a famous German transvestite who survived the Nazi occupation. I memorized ten minutes' worth of the play, acted out all of the parts without props, and used a German accent. I was finally able to display my acting skills. I added comic relief with a monologue from the flamboyantly gay screenwriter, and I made myself cry while acting out axe murdering my abusive Nazi father. I did so well that Ms. Bray asked me to perform it for her speech and debate class the following year as an example of how dramatic interp was done. Matthew was in that class. I didn't notice—I was too busy pistol-whipping the SS.

After my smile comment junior year, Matthew and I started a MySpace romance. Even though we went to the same school, the Internet allowed us to be in constant contact. He added me. I accepted. We commented. We chatted. We messaged. Phone numbers were exchanged. I was so nervous being on the phone with him that all I could talk about was politics. I figured if I was going to ramble, it might as well be about current events. That's why he was at the tournament, right? Not really. The tournament where we met was his one mandated tournament to pass the class. Despite his lack of interest, however, he was smarter than the average sophomore and held his own during my liberal rants.

I didn't have anywhere to go that New Year's Eve. Matthew really wanted to get me to a party. He failed at that. Instead we chatted all night. In the morning we figured he could bus from Vancouver down to my mom's house in Portland. We met at Starbucks. When he arrived, I couldn't understand why a guy so attractive was interested in me. We hugged. We talked about the quote on my coffee cup and the Morgan Freeman look-alike he saw on the bus. We didn't want our time together to end.

We didn't let it end. We smoked and walked to my grand-parents' basement. I wanted to watch *Casablanca*, but I couldn't find it, so I put on *A Bit of Fry and Laurie*. You'd be surprised how romantic eighties British sketch comedy can be. I finally understood how amazing a kiss could be. When it's with the right person, it sweeps you up into a dimension of pure passion. I was so happy I wanted to cry.

But he had to leave.

The following week, we had an overnight tournament at the University of Puget Sound in Seattle. He had already completed his mandatory single tournament, but competed in extemporaneous speaking to be with me. I got to spend hours with him. Why is it that all I can remember about the dialogue was that it was perfect? The only thing that wasn't perfect was all the other people.

My former best friends in speech and debate had been slowly phasing me out of their group. This had happened to me before, in the eighth grade. But by junior year, I assumed we were all too mature for this, especially Briana. She was the reason I stayed in speech and debate. She had a sick sense of humor. She had a crazy style. Briana was great at crafts and clothesmaking. She made her first oratory about vegetarianism, and knew pop-culture references that went over even my head. She had a lovely dysfunctional family. Briana seemed to be above all drama. But then she proved me wrong.

We had been instant friends in ninth grade, but I may have idolized her too much, because by junior year, she was sick of me being a bummer. She made it clear to me that I should be getting over my rape much more quickly than I was. She was taciturn and perpetually irritated with me, and she helped turn Alex and Jenni, fellow tournament regulars, that way, too. I wasn't looking forward to sharing a room with them in Seattle. But they weren't the only bad part of that trip.

When I got there, I realized I had forgotten my script. I had it memorized, but for my particular event, you have to mimic the act of reading. I was disqualified. I was disappointed and humiliated. Matthew was lovely, though. We had fun just hanging out between his rounds.

My roommates got back to the hotel and went to sleep. Briana had a cot, Jenni and Alex shared a bed, and I shared a bed with Allison, a tournament regular who wasn't part of our clique. Because I had a cold, I was snoring. Jenni and Alex started throwing things at me.

"What?"

"You're snoring."

"Sorry."

They continued throwing things but heavier objects, remotes, and shoes. I woke up with bruises. As if they need physical violence to make me feel unwanted.

We went to the second day of the tournament, where I sat twiddling my thumbs again. Then Matthew and I wandered over to a certain section of the campus where an adult, a coach or a judge, was hypnotizing teenage girls to orgasm on command. I was horrified. This type of thing would already be outrageous to me as a feminist, but I was in the middle of my rape trial, and Matthew was the first boy I'd had any interest in since Frank. I was overwhelmed. This was the last straw. Or so I thought.

When we got back to the room, I was sick, tired, humiliated, and fragile. Then Briana and the girls ever so politely suggested that I spend the night with Matthew in his room instead of with them. I put on my shoes and walked down to the lobby. They thought the worst and assumed I was running away or doing something rash. All I wanted to do was to cool down from the rejection and hurt I felt and return when they were asleep.

They called my cell phone, bitching about my leaving and yelling at me to get back to the room. I told them to fuck off. A teammate was on the other side of the lobby, and when I heard him on his cell phone telling them where I was, I walked outside. I didn't want them following me. I wanted to be alone, to breathe, and to call my parents. I called them, sobbing, begging them to pick me up. They said they would try. Then my phone died.

I went back upstairs, petrified to face those girls again. All I could think to do was to knock on Ms. Bray's door. I thought she'd be sympathetic. I was wrong there, too. Of course I was disturbing her, but I was desperate.

"Hannah, you cannot just come crying into my room in the middle of the night."

She walked me back to my room, listened as three against one gave their stories, and told us to go to bed. The next morning, Ms. Bray drove Matthew and me home in one of the vans. Matthew told me how scared he was that I was breaking up with him, that he was the reason I had walked out of the room. He thought I thought he wanted to pressure me into having sex because he was receptive to the idea of sleeping in the same bed. I told him that wasn't it at all. Not even close. I fell asleep on his shoulder. I woke up at my house.

"Was I snoring?"

"Yeah, but it was a cute snore."

I stepped out of the van and twisted my ankle. Matthew and my dad helped me into the house. I thought my clumsy exit summarized the trip pretty well; however, the humiliation wasn't over.

The next day at school, Ms. Bray called a meeting to discuss disciplinary actions. I decided not to try to defend myself, but instead sat silent, saying "I'm sorry" repeatedly. Everyone agreed that the biggest offense of the evening was my leaving the hotel. That the others had thrown shoes and remotes at me wasn't ignored, but not a single person fought on my side. Ms. Bray said we couldn't go to National Qualifiers because of a) the way we all behaved, and b) we had no money. What everyone heard was: *Hannah is the reason we're not going.* They made no effort to hide that. Matthew sat quietly, holding my hand.

On my walk home that afternoon, I ran into Briana's older brother, Jake, the mohawked druggie who was on our team before he transferred to alternative school. I thought he was friendly. He even chatted casually with me at first. I asked him what he was doing there.

"I'm going to talk to Bray."

"Oh, about what?"

"About how the team shouldn't be punished for your stupid actions."

"Excuse me?"

"I've seen you. You're a fucking drama queen. You fuck up shit just to get attention. I remember in the van ride last year when you were annoying us all with your crying and you were clearly forcing yourself to prolong it."

"Dude, I can't physically help it! I hadn't eaten in days, my medication was all fucked up, I hadn't slept because *you* kept me up all night fooling around with Alex and Jenni. If I tried to keep myself from crying I would've . . . I don't know . . . thrown up or something."

"*Then fucking throw up next time!*"

Obviously, he was right. I was a waste of molecules. How had Matthew not realized that yet?

* * *

On Valentine's Day, a few weeks later, I walked into the student center to grab breakfast, and there on the table was a heart-shaped cake with frosting spelling out MATTHEW + HANNAH. There was also a sweetheart teddy bear, an I Love

You balloon, and a card that said Hannah Westburg. I laughed out loud at the misspelling of my last name. Lunch ladies and secretaries teased me. I opened the card and it started singing "Don't Worry, Be Happy." I read the card: "If your heart is light and happy then my Valentine wish has come true . . . and my heart will be happy too!" He had written on the other side: "So I wasn't particularly fond of the cheesy poem on the card, but the song was nice so I got it! Hmmm . . . what to do with all this space left? Oh! I got an idea! (lightbulb) I LOVE YOU, HANNAH!" Not bad. He filled up the rest of the space with a big heart.

Out of the card fell a note. One side said, "Matthew loves the Hannah." The other side had a small heart with a larger heart drawn around it: the small heart said "before," the larger heart said "after." It read: "In case you were wondering, this is my heart. Thanks to you, it has stretch marks." The inside of the note was an additional full page featuring several mushy declarations of his monumental, life-changing love for me. He ended it with a smiley face.

How could something so beautiful turn so ugly in three months?

The day after Valentine's Day, I dragged him to see *The Vagina Monologues*, which plays around V-Day every year. I wore a new dress. Without any prompting he called me beautiful. I honestly thought he would enjoy the play and we could share my passion for feminism a little. Unfortunately, this plan was ruined because the production was horrible.

We went to the closest production playing, which happened to be at the local community college. We joked around at first, I flirtatiously licked the chocolate vagina lollipop he bought me, and then the show started. They had a stupid gym motif. They added a theme where there already was one. The performances were forced and unimaginative. I've seen three other productions and this was by far the worst.

They butchered it, but I still felt that Matthew should have been slightly moved by the script or at least pretended to be. He wasn't impressed and he let it show. We sat in silence, waiting for his mom to pick us up. We wanted to go to dinner, too, because this was our first official date, but we ended up driving through Taco Bell. I paid because he bought the tickets. I went home and Matthew went to Burgerville to visit his cousin.

We had never fought before that. It wasn't even a fight, it was a misunderstanding that turned into passive-aggressive silence. In retrospect, I know the night could've been saved. But I was too stubborn. Luckily, this isn't what broke us up.

We spent every waking moment together or talking on the phone, but it wasn't quite enough for him. I would invite him out whenever I was with my friends, but then he would say we didn't have enough alone time. It wasn't that I didn't want to be with him, it was that I didn't have any more time to give. We almost never had anywhere to go. When my parents weren't home, we had to hang out on the porch. We still had wonderful times. Our rapport only got better. He cried on my shoulder when his stepdad punched him in the face, and I cried on his shoulder when my parents kicked me out. We were about to buy each other promise rings. That's why I was so shocked by what happened.

He came over to my house one day. He sat down and told me that he couldn't handle being in a relationship with me anymore because his mom was dying and he might be moving. I wanted to be understanding and keep my cool, but I ended up desperate. I sent him off, truly believing that we would stay friends. We returned each other's blankets. I didn't let him see me cry.

I wrote a MySpace blog and kept updating it with each new emotion. It started out private, but I ended up changing the settings to allow a few good friends to read it. I wrote about how he expected me to trust him never to leave but he couldn't trust me to be there for him while his mom was dying. A friend told me how Matthew was telling his friends he was breaking up with me for different reasons. I imagined that it was because I was fat and ugly, that I hadn't gone all the way with him, or that he liked Becca, a mutual friend of ours. The only logical explanation I came up with was because I wouldn't fully commit to him. I wrote on my blog that it was horrible if he had used his mom's dying as an excuse to break up with me. Becca misunderstood this and told Matthew that I said he lied about his mother dying and that I wished his mom dead. He wrote me a scathing letter and wouldn't give me the benefit of the doubt, even after I convinced Becca that she had read my blog wrong. Our potential friendship ended abruptly with horrible anger. Hating him didn't make me love him any less.

I got rid of reminders of him. I mentioned him less often. I thought of him more as a memory and less as a longing. I dated other guys. I got over him. I haven't had a relationship as serious since. A large part of that is due to long periods of isolation or having no time. Another part of that is how safe Matthew made me feel. I tried not to trust him, having been let down before, but through all of his I love yous and talk about our getting married and having a life together, I started to believe it, too. This may have been par for the course for him. He's engaged now. Many of my eighteen-year-old friends are, or married with kids even. I know the marriages won't last. He taught me that lesson. It's not cynicism. It means when I do commit to someone, it'll be based wisely on a solid foundation, and it'll mean so much more.

Diagnosis

MY CITY IS SWARMING WITH UNIQUENESS. The Portland streets are filled with hipsters and indies, and they are all special. I have to work hard just to keep up. I want my style to tell people how great I am before I get the chance to open my mouth and ruin the illusion.

My mom gave me bus fair and a few extra dollars to go shopping in the hip Hawthorne district. My suburban high school across the river might accept and even encourage average dress, but this was different. I didn't want to be forgettable. I ended up in pedal pushers, a polka-dotted blouse, rhinestone glasses, and red, red lipstick. I made my look just modern enough so that it was ironic retro, not a costume. I was fully aware of how pretentious I was being, glad people couldn't hear my thoughts.

I strutted through the vintage clothing stores, looked at the witty, topical gifts in the shops, bought a coffee so intricate it took longer to order than to drink. I ended up bored, as apathetic people often do, and took the bus downtown. I went to the bookstore, the one that's bigger than the Strand, that takes up a whole city block. Every true Portlander has gotten lost in Powell's, the city of books.

Unfortunately, this landmark is in the middle of a scary part of town. When I get overly confident, I forget that I'm a vulnerable young girl. I think I've seen it all, and then I see a battered woman barely conscious in the bus shelter. She was passed out on the sidewalk, either from her injuries or drugs. It occurred to me that this might not even be her rock bottom. I had a long way down to go. I called 9-1-1 and waited with her, all the while seeing my potential future in her bloodied face.

I wanted to go home, fall back on reliable comfort, but I took the wrong bus. It was dark and I didn't realize it was going the opposite direction. I did not want to be stranded on a bus going nowhere in the middle of the night after what

I just saw. My fingers grazed the baggie in my purse that contained my tools of razors and pills. I had gotten into the habit of carrying them with me like a security blanket. I got off at a hospital at the edge of town. As I waited for the right bus to come, I smoked a cigarette and contemplated how my Ziploc of self-destruction could lead to being passed out on the sidewalk; how when I thought I just wanted to run away from my life, hit bottom hard, and become a homeless crack whore, I had no idea what I was dealing with. I threw the bag into the trash and got on the bus.

A homeless man on the bus was clearly deaf and having trouble communicating with anyone. We ended up waiting at the same bus stop when we got off the first bus. I started finger-spelling and using my limited knowledge of sign language to make small talk. I tend to try to humanize interactions like this instead of just dropping coins into outstretched hands and walking away.

He pulled out a notepad and after a few minutes of chit-chat wrote "$20?"

"For what?" I wrote. I thought he wanted my money.

"Like, sex?" he wrote.

I did the sign for an adamant "No!" and walked away. He got on his bike and rode away. I got on my bus.

What about me led him to believe I was a prostitute? Because I was out at 10 PM? Did my attempt at retro turn out slutty? Was I being punished for being friendly?

I didn't have a chance to think this through before he got on the bus a few blocks down. He had just ridden his bike to the next stop. I asked a woman to sit next to me for the duration and asked the bus driver not to let him out at my stop. I was still terrified. Maybe if I knew what I had done to make him believe my body was for sale, I wouldn't have started running. Nighttime and heels are a deadly combination. I didn't have a coat that matched my outfit—I also thought I'd be home by eight. I was left shivering in the darkness, wishing I hadn't thrown away my tools, for they would have helped me atone for whatever I did to deserve this. I was left wishing that I hadn't let my clothes or my wounds speak for me for all this time.

I got back to my mom's apartment safe and sound. I had some comfort food and went to sleep. I woke up the next morning out of danger, but feeling vulnerable without my weapons, though I would only have used them on myself.

With or without my vices, I felt like I was reaching the end of my rope. I was going crazy waiting for the next antidepressants to kick in. I couldn't remember what was keeping me going. I was going through the motions. Somehow I kept waking up day after day, sure that this would be my last brush with disaster.

One afternoon, I got on the train to go to my therapist's office. I'd started seeing my therapist Aniko after my stay at the Children's Farm Home and had been seeing her ever since. That day I was as depressed as I've ever been, and someone with no pants got on the train. Then more people got on wearing just shirts and underwear. There were about thirty people now, and more came on at each stop: women in their panties and men in their boxers. I couldn't believe it. I was in the middle of a hilariously baffling flash mob.

By the time I had arrived at my therapist's office, I was ecstatic. "I was so depressed, so unbelievably ready to end it all, and then this happened," I said. "Life is just too fucking ridiculous to miss!"

* * *

The flash mob event gave me an emotional boost; it helped me see things differently, at least for a while. On top of that, I had transferred to an alternative school in eleventh grade and did great that first semester. I got As and won student awards. I went on school trips to the museum and the beach. I painted a self-portrait and got an essay published. I made friends, went to parties, and went to prom in a beautiful dress. I got second place as a youth fundraiser for AIDS Walk, mostly through donations from teachers who loved me. Then senior year came around and everything went downhill.

In the middle of that year, Aniko decided she had taught me all she could and it was time for me to use my skills on my own, without the crutch of a weekly session. She put plenty of time and energy easing me into the transition, but this was during, perhaps not so coincidentally, the longest period of depression I had ever experienced. Not only that, but the way I was behaving suggested there was more than just depression going on, something that couldn't necessarily be fixed with a pill.

The combination of my rape case and losing Aniko and Matthew left me completely lost. I fell into old habits. I relapsed with everything. I was cutting habitually again. Prior to this, I'd had a handful of one-time relapses, but something about having to answer to Aniko kept it from happening again. But this time, I even relapsed with pills, something I hadn't had a problem with since ninth grade. I regressed into my fourteen-year-old self. Depression made me slow and I needed speed. I needed it to function. So I stole Ritalin that was prescribed to my mom and dad. It was so bad that I was snorting the pills in the school bathroom. That is, when I wasn't purging.

When I was in school, I was a zombie. I did nothing, so my only options were independent study or getting my GED. I chose the former. I did well for the first week, and then when I sat down to do my homework, I would just stare at the computer screen. I would do that for a while before giving up and watching TV and sleeping. I never officially dropped out . . . I just stopped showing up. I would often sneak out at night to go to a diner with some friends. We weren't doing anything bad, except when I would duck into the bathroom to do a line and then come back to the table, sniffing and chattering. If I didn't, then I couldn't get through a conversation. I would just go home and sleep all day.

Sometimes I would sneak out at night to meet up with a friend, Sean. Our friendship was based on my exploiting his vices so I could be self-destructive. We walked around on amphetamines all night. We got drunk at his place and he tried to make a move on me. We got into the back of his friend's truck and took hits off the pipe that everyone was passing around, including the driver. I smoked so much pot that night that I lost touch with reality. I sneaked back into my house and went to sleep, only to wake up screaming an hour later. For fifteen minutes I screamed at the top of my lungs. I knew I needed help, even though I didn't understand what help meant. I couldn't believe that my parents didn't hear me. I crawled into the hallway and kept screaming. Dad and Carol finally came down the stairs. Dad held me while I blubbered nonsense like, "Pain wasn't real and faces weren't faces!" Carol was unimpressed.

In fact, Carol was sick of me. She didn't want to acknowledge that my depression could be so debilitating—she felt she was the one in the most pain. One night when I was searching their room for pills or alcohol, I found a book. The title was all I needed to see—*Stop Walking on Eggshells: Taking Your Life Back When Someone You Care About Has Borderline Personality Disorder.*

I became furious. *How dare she be so demeaning as to put this label on me? Is she a fucking psychiatrist? No. She just can't deal with the fact that I don't take her shit anymore. The Children's Farm Home psychiatrist said I fit the diagnostic criteria but I was too young to be diagnosed with it, so clearly, I don't have it. I'm not crazy. I just have depression. Besides, even if I did have borderline personality disorder, that would be* my *problem! Why does she always have to be the martyr? Just because I don't let her walk all over me anymore doesn't mean I'm taking her life away. Walking on eggshells? Please! More like being a perpetual bitch since the day we met.*

That's how I saw it, anyway. I didn't know at the time I was being typical borderline with my black-and-white-you're-with-me-or-you're-against-me, all-or-nothing thinking. I was hostile and willful. My parents were my enemies and I let them know it by breaking their things and leaving glass shards everywhere. I was doing the borderline thing by manipulating my parents and daring them not to abandon me.

So I started researching and discovered that drugs, cutting, and obsessive eating, or lack thereof, were all classic symptoms of borderline personality disorder. All this time, my self-hatred and suicide attempts weren't just depression. The helplessness, hopelessness, worthlessness, guilt, anger, anxiety, loneliness, boredom, and emptiness I experienced— things I had taken to be a fact of my life—were all symptoms of something bigger.

I read through the description online and saw the story of myself begin to take shape. I said "Yep" to each bullet point. Finally, even though I hated the label, especially since borderlines are notoriously the most obnoxious of mental patients, I accepted the diagnosis. I was annoyed with myself when I realized that most of my self-destruction was attention seeking after all. It had taken until I was an adult for each aspect to fully emerge, but luckily, the form of therapy I was already using—DBT—was designed for borderline patients, so I had the skills to deal with it. I knew I had to accept the disease if I were to find a cure.

Symptoms reveal themselves to this day, through new experiences and retrospective epiphanies. I have intense and unstable relationships. I realized that almost all of my anger toward my parents was inappropriate and based on subtle slights: classic BPD. I counted up how many people I've kissed and realized that most of those kisses were the result of my loneliness, insecurity, need for validation, and my ability to read nonexistent body language. I willingly had sex with someone for the first time when I was drunk and literally beat myself up when he rejected me, and then I slept with him three more times. I slept with another guy a few weeks later and started an unofficial relationship with him. Then when I thought he was losing interest, I made out with someone else in front of him. When I ran after him sobbing, I knew I wanted to apologize, but I couldn't think of what could've possibly made me do such an ugly and hurtful thing. I was frantically avoiding imagined abandonment.

The clarifying moment for me was when I came back from a trip to San Francisco to visit Nicole. We had texted so much before the trip, mostly when she was feeling lonely and isolated. But when I got back home, she was so busy with school that she was texting less. I freaked out. I was sure this meant she hated me and that I was all alone in the world. I couldn't get the paranoia out of my head. I felt truly crazy. It was horrible.

Since that event, I'm working on recognizing when I'm in that space, and I'm trying to keep myself from going to a dark emotional place with DBT skills and balancing my thoughts. Even though I know how to keep getting up each time, I still fall. But at least I'm confident that I will always stand up again.

Relapse

NICOLE AND TONY HAD LOCKED themselves in their room again. I'm unnecessary during that part of the vacation. Tony had driven me down to San Francisco to visit Nicole at college. When we were just hanging out, visiting Haight-Ashbury, the Pier, Ghirardelli Square, walking around campus, Black Friday shopping, we got along great. Occasionally they would get romantic and I felt extraneous, but mostly we were a tricycle. We got BFF bracelets at the arcade. We had instant inside jokes. But there was no denying that sometimes I was crashing their relationship. Now they were behind closed doors again. It didn't mean they had stopped loving me. But it could've meant that I would be alone forever.

Just a little slice. No one has to know about it. It'll barely bleed. Maybe I'll take another shot first. No, the cutting will be enough to make me feel better. The knife is too dull. I could just stab it. Wow, that's a lot of blood. I don't want to die because I cut too deep while I was drunk. Maybe I'll just wait and see if it clots soon. No, this is gushing out with my heartbeat. I have to tell them.

"Tony . . . I did something bad."

"What did you do?"

"Um, something bad . . ."

"What did you do?"

"But you have to promise not to freak out."

"Show me your wrist."

"It's not my wrist, it's my thigh." Oops.

I heard his heavy sigh through the closed door. "I'll be out in a couple minutes."

I'm still bleeding. Maybe I'll just go out to the balcony and get some fresh air. Oh, look, there are boys stumbling around the campus. Maybe if I sleep with someone and get a boyfriend I won't feel so useless.

"Hey, boys!"

"Hey, girl!"

"You drunk?"

"Yeah."

"Me, too. I'll let you sleep with me."

"Really?"

"Yeah."

"Let us up."

"Okay, I'll be right down."

I rode the elevator down, giggling about the blood on my pajama pants. When I opened the door, one of the guys burst through and started kissing me. I looked at his face . . . he seemed cute at the time. Not that I consider myself any sort of prize. He was grabbing my ass. I pressed the button for the elevator.

"Hey, you should let me take pictures of me doing anal on you."

"No way!"

"It's for my frat. You know what frat I'm getting into?"

I asked and he told me.

Then I realized, "I don't care!"

We stumbled into the elevator. He was grabbing my

breasts. He started fingering me over my pants. His hands were on my ass again when Tony walked in.

He explained to them that they should leave. I giggled while I repeatedly said, "I'm sorry." He paused and then punched the metal wall, hard. He walked me down to Nicole's door and told me to wait outside for Nicole. She had the key. He went looking for her.

She arrived and let me in. I saw the blood on the floor and the disappointment in her eyes. I didn't know what the big fuss was about. She should've known by then that I was a consistent fuck-up.

Nicole tried to put Band-Aids on my wound, but I kept getting up. "Why are the boys in the living room? I should go apologize." Nicole just shut the door and sat me back down.

"Hey, Hannah, which one were you making out with?"

"Um, he's wearing a green shirt and he's Asian and he's cute. I should go apologize."

She sat me down, walked out the bedroom door and over to the common room couch, and slapped him in the face. The boys left.

"Dude, why would you slap him? He didn't do anything."

"I know, but it made me feel better."

I wandered over to the couch and commenced my notorious self-deprecating rambling. This was just a repeat of what had happened when I drank too much two nights earlier, only this time had a little less conversation and a little more action.

A few weeks earlier, Nicole had proposed that I drive down to San Francisco with her boyfriend, Tony. I missed her like mad, but more important, she couldn't stand being alone. Her classmates were ignorant partiers. They did nothing but drink and bitch. They overtook the living room, leaving Nicole cooped up in her room, exacerbating her depression. They obsessed over food and calories, even though they were thin, worsening Nicole's anorexic tendencies. She couldn't help but abuse ibuprofen, since her roommates were always giving her headaches. Relieving the pain in her head only gave her pain in her stomach. No one cared about the world at her school. She was miserable.

As soon as Tony and I arrived two nights earlier, I realized how many of her problems might truly be based on her environment. Tony and Nicole had gone to have sex in her room, so I had to wait in the living room with her roommates and a few friends. They were as physically flawless as Nicole had described. It didn't help that I was already feeling left out in a room full of strangers. They kept grilling me for dirt about my best friend. They were drinking and it seemed like the thing to do. I knew being fat around all those superficial skinny girls would be better if I were a little drunk.

I only meant to calm my nerves a little, but the beer and the two shots weren't kicking in fast enough. I had two more shots and went to the balcony to smoke some pot. As always, I held my smoke in way too long. I don't know how many times I puff puff passed, but I felt as if I was in another dimension. Time wasn't connected, everything in the world was assigned a number. Everything was strange, but I was okay with it. Eventually, I went to bed.

I woke up to a slap in the face. It was the only way Tony could shake me from my night terror. Apparently, I was squirming and whimpering, which slowly turned into screams. I'd had night terrors before—I woke up screaming, crying, and terrified—but this time, I just woke up amused.

I was still in my other dimension. I was swaying uncontrollably, my legs were between the boards in the bed, and I was being tossed between Nicole, who was sitting behind me, and Tony, who was holding my arms in front of me. I may have tried to weakly hit him when I woke up. But slowly, the dimensions faded away. I was still blathering, repeating the same things over and over. It wasn't just recovery from a night terror—I was still high and emotionally vulnerable.

Tony decided I couldn't go to sleep like that. We moved out to the living room. My inhibitions were lowered enough that my suicidal tendencies were revealed. I kept walking out to the balcony to lean over the railing and see where the hard ground four stories below could crack my skull open.

"Why am I even alive, dude? I mean, I don't want to kill myself. But why am I alive? I should've never been born. I mean, why would you give birth to someone and then try to kill yourself? If my mom didn't want me that much, she should've never had me. And what did I do that was so bad that Carol wanted to leave me all the time? Was I really that bad? It's because I'm a bad person. I'm pure evil. I'm as bad as Hitler or Bush. I do more bad in the world than good.

Everyone hates me. I'm Jabba the Hut fat and freak show ugly and you guys can't even stand to look at me right now, right? Dude, what the fuck are all these scars? Do these really accomplish anything? No, but cutting really does make me feel better. I hate my life and I hate myself, and I swear I'm not going to kill myself, but I probably should, right?"

As if this weren't bad enough, this speech was repeated several times with responses demanded. I listed every traumatic experience I'd had so they would know that this breakdown was well deserved. They took turns reassuring me, telling me they had already covered why I shouldn't kill myself, providing soothing answers to my rhetorical questions.

Nicole eventually fell asleep. Tony was there when I sobered up a little.

"Hannah, you need to stay alive because Nicole needs a best friend. Do you know what it would do to her if you left?"

"I'm just worried that I'm a bad person and that it would be better for the earth if I wasn't here."

"How could that possibly be true?"

"Well, don't you think I'm going to hell?"

"In Mormonism, there are three different places you can

go in the afterlife. One is for the truly bad people—the Hitlers and Bushes. One is for nonbelievers that are still good people. One is for the really devout religious ones. You would go into the second one. I don't think that God, in all of His infinite wisdom, would ignore how much you care about people and how much selfless good you do just because you don't go to church and you've made a few mistakes."

"I think I've always, in the back of my mind, believed in God. Whether it's just because I was raised on it or what, I can't stop believing in God. I was just so scared of rejection. I ignored Him because I thought He wouldn't like me," I said.

Then we prayed together. He prayed for me and he prayed for himself. Then we went to bed and I prayed. I cried and I prayed. I had missed Him so much. Then I fell asleep.

Two nights later, when I was running around making out with strangers and leaving a trail of blood from the gash on my leg, Nicole was sneaking shots. Then she started cleaning and organizing everything she could find. When I noticed she had been gone for a while, I found her in the bathroom trying to dry a piece of paper with a towel, and sobbing.

"It isn't supposed to be wet!" she said.

"What is it?"

"I don't know, but it's not supposed to be wet!"

"That's okay. Give it to me; come here."

She was crying on my shoulder while I squeezed her.

"Here, come sit with me."

"No, I have to go count the dishes."

I closed the door and pulled her down.

"No, you don't. It's okay."

"But they're not even!"

"That's okay if they're not even. The world is more beautiful when it's uneven."

"But I need things to be symmetrical!"

"Do you know how bored I would be by your photography if it were symmetrical?"

"I'm never gonna be a photographer. I'm no good at anything. I should just be dead."

"If you're dead, you can't travel the world and capture its beauty. You can't marry Tony and have kids and run a coffee shop. You can't do Pilates with me. They don't let dead people tour the Shanghai tunnels and we still have to do that."

"I need to go make the dishes even."

We sat on the floor, repeating ourselves until she stopped crying. I stroked her arms and her hair evenly on both sides. Tony and I got her to bed. She got up only once to count the dishes. Eventually, we went to sleep.

After that first night of the trip, when I had been rambling about suicide, it was easier to wake up the next morning and face the music. After that first night I could joke about it—all I needed was some Tylenol and to wear my sunglasses. But this time was harder.

Tony got up a little after I did and asked me if I wanted to go with him to get a parking pass. I wanted to crawl into a shame-hole, but I wasn't about to say no to Tony, my savior, for anything. When we got to the elevator, we tentatively chuckled about the damage he had done when he'd punched the wall the night before. My hopes that my memory of what had gone down was mostly a dream were dashed. I was afraid to say anything. He was trying to be casual, making small talk, presumably to make me comfortable, but I was still convinced that he hated me. I knew I hated me.

"You know, Tony, I'm really not a danger to myself. At all. I swear."

"I know that. I mean, I thought you were last night."

"Well, you don't have to worry about that. Besides, I learned that one reason why I go a little nuts in the evening is because my antidepressants leave my body ridiculously quickly, so I can't forget to take the nighttime dose."

"I'm just really worried about Nicole. She feels bad, just, *all* of the time. I don't know what I can do."

"All you can do is be there, be supportive. For the record, I think you're doing a really great job. Nicole is pretty new to the therapeutic process. I know that after a relapse, I have the tools to get right back on that horse, but I'm not totally sure she does."

As it turned out, she did. We were making sick jokes about our mental breakdowns that occurred within a few hours of each other. We were mentally fragile, but fine. My only problems at that point were physical.

It started out as rocking. I thought it was gentle rocking for comfort, but my legs began shaking more violently. Then the shaking in my hands turned into uncontrollable movement. I drank some water, thinking it was hangover dehydration. Tony made some food, but I had no appetite and ate only a few bites. The shaking stopped then started up again.

"Eat your frickin' food!"

"I'm fine."

"Yeah, you look fine."

"Maybe I just need a vitamin."

It worked. My vitamins replenished, I could stop shaking and we could go out for Thanksgiving Chinese, wearing my sunglasses, of course.

Afterward, I pulled Nicole aside. "Hey, guess what? I now have a real, concrete reason not to cut. Blood loss makes you twitch uncontrollably. Plus, I have a heinous bruise around the wound. That can't be good."

"Yeah, what's my concrete reason not to count dishes?"

"Um . . . you end up crying on the bathroom floor?"

"Good point."

"So the good thing is that at least we learned something from our breakdowns."

"There was nothing good about your mental break-downs!" Tony shouted.

Simultaneously, Nicole and I shouted back, "Shut up! You're not a part of this!"

We smiled at each other. We were closer than ever. I felt a part of something again.

Growing Up

CAROL STOPPED TALKING TO ME. She simply stated one day that she wasn't going to speak to me anymore. To her, this was a solution, a way to save herself from the wreckage that was Hannah. To me, this was just a new, creative form of abandonment. She disowned me while we were still living in the same house. This only made me want to break more things. I broke my skin with a razor yet again.

In an emergency family therapy session, we aired our issues. Apparently Carol loves me. I told her she had to stop threatening to leave, because I have abandonment issues stemming from my mother's absences. She agreed, but she still told me I had to move out.

I was eighteen. I had just gotten my GED. Taking that

test had been the first productive thing I'd done since my most recent bout of depression had started. Now, my dad and Carol told me they wanted me to gain independence. They thought that if I could no longer count on them to provide for me, I would be motivated to get on with my life.

I had gotten a job with Children International the day before my dad broke the news to me. We were in the car on the way to my mom's when he told me. I burst out crying. I had barely touched adulthood. After one day of standing on the street in the hot sun, fruitlessly asking people to sponsor a child, I was fired. I cried on the bus the whole way home. I felt destined to be homeless.

I kept up my job search but felt constantly defeated in the midst of the economic recession. Both Carol and Dad were unemployed, and I felt it was unreasonable for them to expect me to support myself when I had no job experience and my resume was blank. I filled out over a hundred job applications but had no response. I went back to my old ways of falling asleep in front of the television.

At least Nevada and Sarah had been able to live in my grandparents' basement while they were in college and just after graduation. But this option was out for me because my aunt Naomi had cancer and spent substantial periods of time recuperating there, and her son, Leo, ended up moving in instead. Grandpa got Leo a job working for his colleague and gave him his car. Needless to say, I was jealous. I was convinced that as soon as Dad and Carol kicked me out, I would either be couch surfing, in a youth transitional (homeless) shelter, or paying $100 a month to live in Tony's freezing cold garage.

My parents told me I had to be out by August. I got into a few dramatic arguments with them about how lost I felt and how unreasonable they were being. Carol kept saying she wanted to finally start her life alone with my father. In my eyes, this wasn't about me finding independence—it was about Carol getting rid of me.

I was still living with them when I got a regular babysitting gig. It never paid very well. Even if I had gotten one of those government checks the young mother promised me, it still wouldn't have added up to minimum wage. I loved helping out a low-income teenage mom and I loved her cute little baby, but it was no career. Dad and Carol got way too excited about it. They thought I could live off it, so they began pushing me out the door.

The temp agency I had signed up with months earlier suddenly had an assignment for me. I was babysitting when I got the call. Two seconds after the teenage mom's aunt picked up the baby, Dad and I raced off so I could take a drug test, and I met a representative from the temp agency at a Wendy's an hour later to sign the paperwork. I started work at the plastics factory that night at 11 PM. The graveyard shift paid $9.50 an hour for forty hours a week. If I was better at the job than the other two temps, I would get hired permanently. To me, this meant not being homeless. I was positive that I would beat out the others because I needed it more. Just in case, though, I decided to keep babysitting for the next two weeks until I knew I got the job.

The first day was fine. It was mostly taking plastic parts out of machines, checking for flaws, and packaging them with paperwork, then sweeping the floors at the end of the day. I used my semiphotographic memory to sing eight hours of memorized song lyrics. I stayed overly enthusiastic in order to stand apart.

The second day, I was sweeping up with my purse on my hip. When I knelt down to brush the debris into the dustpan, I accidentally switched on a water valve just enough so that it showered on me, like a cartoon rain cloud of sadness over a Looney Tunes character. In a few seconds that lasted a lifetime, I found the switch and shut off the water flow. I got in the car and asked my dad, "Why am I *always* the one doing the stupid, humiliating, clumsy things in front of large crowds?" I went back to work the next night with a forced smile.

By then, I had been up for three days with only six hours of sleep, and when I got to work, they put me on a difficult machine. I have heard descriptions of hell as doing the same impossible task over and over. The fact that the machine was way too fast for me felt like a nightmare in which you have to run away but you're stuck in slow motion. I had to take a part out of the machine, close the door, push the button, wipe off oil, check for flaws, clip off extraneous plastic, test it for uneven edges, cool it, bag it, and put it into the box. By the time I had done all of this, the next part was already waiting for me. If I left it too long, I would set off the alarm. And I did, several times. I had no time to scratch my nose, let alone change boxes, fill out paperwork, and stick on labels—three more things I got lectured about when I couldn't complete them on time.

Coworkers came to help me, and their foreign accents seemed thicker and their broken English became nearly unintelligible. I tried to hold back the tears but I couldn't. My hands were burned and blistered from the previous days and suddenly my plastic parts were getting covered in blood. I looked at my hands and saw that I had gotten cut and didn't notice it. I held up my bloody finger to one of the many people surrounding me. One of the technicians got me a Band-Aid.

The supervisor showed up, so I asked him if I could wash my hands. I'm sure he noticed my red wet eyes under my safety glasses. He told me that we were just making plastic; it was nothing to cry about. I explained it was just sleep deprivation. I went to the bathroom, sank to the floor, and sobbed. I washed the eyeliner running down my cheeks, but there was no getting rid of the puffiness or red splotches. I went back to my machine and did my work in super-speed, praying that I would faint or have a seizure or the machine would crush my head. When I came home, through tears I told Carol what had happened.

"What do you want me to do about it?" she said.

After a couple of seconds of stunned silence, I said, "Nothing, I just wanted a hug." She gave me one and I left.

Nicole told me that her friend Xylia needed a roommate. Her boyfriend was moving out and she couldn't pay the whole rent herself. It was a one-bedroom, but she consented to sleeping on the couch most nights. I agreed immediately to room with her. Carol and Dad cheered at the news. I was excited but scared. I wasn't sure how I would support myself, but I was sick of hearing how Dad and Carol couldn't support me on unemployment and Dad's tips. Mostly I was just tired of hearing how I was keeping Dad and Carol from pursuing their dreams to move out and go on tour or move to Las Vegas, where Dad would be sure to get better paying gigs. Someday they would go to Paris and do nothing but write and act and sing together.

Carol dismantled the extensive collage on my walls and rented out the downstairs the next day, while I was still surrounded by boxes. In the first week, Carol told me to get my address officially changed so I wouldn't get mail there. She had done the same thing to Rachel, but she had let Rachel keep her room and get mail there until she was twenty-one. I would never get to spend another summer, spring break, or Christmas living with my sister in my father's home.

Dad came over to my new place one day with my mail and a handful of quarters. He told me I couldn't go home to do laundry. Dad was often Carol's messenger, but I could tell this was just Carol's way of removing any possible reason for me to be in her house. Even though it actually made more sense to use the laundry in my apartment complex, this was the last straw for me.

I told Dad everything I felt. He defended Carol and thought I was being harsh. He wanted to help in any way he could. I told him that I knew he wasn't abandoning me, but that the things Carol had done to me over the years—the invasions of privacy, the accusations, the threats, the insults— were too much.

"She thinks I'm a slut, I just know it, which hurts so much because she doesn't even believe that what happened to me was rape."

Dad said, "Wow. I understand." He expressed how sorry he was about what happened to me and said that even though Carol may be more inclined to assign coresponsibility than he did, nobody blamed me. He called me a beautiful, strong, smart woman.

I felt better after that talk, but I still had so much hurt, so many unanswered questions surrounding Carol and the way I'd been treated. So I texted my dad the next day and asked why my brother, Nevada, had been able to live with him and Carol rent-free for a month when he was thirty and I wasn't even able to go home to do laundry.

After getting my text, my dad called me and we finally got down to the root issue—Carol hadn't forgiven me for my hostility when I was depressed and exhibiting my borderline characteristics. And she'd been experiencing unintentional, or imagined, hostility ever since.

"Has she ever loved me and felt like my mother?"

"Of course, she loves all you girls. She just never wanted to be a mother and has been waiting to start her life with me."

I kept asking questions over and over again in slightly different ways to get the truth out of him.

"You should talk with her, try to reconcile with her."

I finally said slowly, loudly, through a few tears, "I need you to tell me right now honestly if she *wants* to love me and be my mother before I talk to her. I have serious maternal abandonment issues and I can't reconcile with her again and beg her to love me only to get shut down and disowned again, because I wouldn't be able to handle it. *Do you understand?*"

My dad became quiet. I expected him to say "talk to Carol" again. Instead, he said, "I understand. Okay, I'll talk to her and get back to you."

I went to the mall with Nicole the next day. All my friends have heard about or experienced Carol's bitchiness, but Nicole knew the most. Like my other friends, she had gotten into the habit of stating "Carol's a bitch" whenever I complained about her. I told Nicole everything, and this time she said it over and over, every time I paused in my story.

"Carol's a bitch. We know this. Look, Hannah, I know you've told me all the wonderful things she's done for your family, but to me, the bad things she's done greatly outweigh the good."

"I know . . . I just need to distance myself from her in case Dad tells me that she doesn't want to be my mother."

"Hannah, you're moved out, you're an adult. Why don't you just cut her out of your life already?" she said.

It made sense. No amount of family therapy so far had forced her to be my mother. If I stopped holding that expectation of her, I wouldn't get so hurt. Whether she raised me or not, she never wanted to be obligated to me and only wanted my father. It was foolish of me to think of myself as her daughter. Neither of my maternal figures were emotionally able to mother me entirely. Wishing they would has only disappointed me. I decided to close the door on Carol. At least for now.

As for my biological mom, she went into the hospital again around the same time I moved out of Dad and Carol's place. There had been a period of years when her medication worked and she stayed out of the hospital. For the past few years though, since she went off that medication because it affected her white blood count, she's been in and out of the hospital as frequently as when I was little.

Her mental illness has left her with no friends, and her

job situation suffers with her fluctuating health. Her absences due to depression, carpal tunnel, or feeling the effects of her Hepatitis C made her lose her job, which depressed her even more. I know that my visits were one of the only things she lived for at some points. For a while, even my being there wasn't doing her any good because I became agitated with her manic behavior and her depressing complaints about her life.

Even though I loved her, I couldn't handle the burden. I visited less and less. I felt immense guilt when she went into the hospital. The doctors told her that she could come home early if someone was there to stay with her. She called me, pretty much asking if I would be her designated suicide watcher for a few days. I had to say no because I had to work. I spent eight hours doing one task with a plastic piece, and instead of singing through it, I blamed myself for her possible death.

But she didn't kill herself. She had to rely on herself and she made it. I did the same thing. Over the past few months, I'd wanted to relapse and was certain I would, but I made it through.

At work, they gave me a toolbox with an X-Acto knife in it. Aniko once suggested that I practice handling tools I used for cutting and using them for their original purposes. I would pick up a pair of scissors and be mindful of passing urges each time I used it. I would shave my legs and be mindful of the razor doing what it was supposed to do. Now, I open my toolbox every day and see the blades of the X-Acto knife. And each day it gets a little easier to leave them there. I'm getting used to using them only to cut plastic. I keep facing challenges, little and big, every day. Even if I fail, I'm still alive. All I have to do is keep on waking up every morning.

Epilogue

I've written right up to the present. I'm nineteen, still growing, learning, and striving for balance. My temp assignment at the plastics factory ended just as I had grown to love it. I'm currently babysitting, broke, and job hunting. However, I am one summer away from starting college.

My plan is to go to community college in two years to be certified as a drug and alcohol counselor. Classes like English and psychology, if not directly about addiction, are interesting and relevant. And I'll also get to do actual in-the-field counseling for credit. At the same time, I'll be taking required courses so I can transfer to a four-year college and work as a counselor while I get my bachelor's degree. I got the idea from people complimenting me on my ability to listen and give advice. I was spurred on by the fact that I don't trust counselors who haven't been through it themselves. I have always dreamed of becoming stable and being able to tell others of the light at the end of the tunnel. That's what I hope I'm doing with this book.

I hardly ever do anything artistic anymore. I might go back to drawing and painting one day, but for now, writing is my only outlet. Reading is definitely a hobby when I have the time or energy, but for the time being, TV and movies have taken over. I like keeping up with politics and raising awareness, and volunteering when I can. I enjoy my music, Facebook, and shopping. Every once in a while I do things like go to the beach, camping, book readings, galleries, plays, concerts, dance clubs, and craft parties. Recently, my neighbor Jackie, with whom I spend most of my time these days, took me to an outdoor rave and her fiancé taught me how to spin poi and dance with glow sticks. I date and it has its ups and downs and breakdowns, of course. I generally like my life.

My roommate and I are still getting used to the dynamic of living together. I have my complaints, but it's nice to be independent. *Hmm, maybe my parents were onto something.* My parents haven't moved yet. They still don't know what they're doing, so I have no idea what Christmas will be like. Nevada lives in Portland, works at the temp agency, and accompanies my dad, so I still talk to him and see him occasionally. Sarah lives with her girlfriend in Portland, is a Starbucks barista, and is on her way to being a sign language interpreter. Rachel is a junior at Evergreen State and majors in women's studies. Even though she's in Olympia, we're on Facebook so much that she feels closer than my siblings in Portland.

Nicole ended up hating CSU, so she lives at home and goes to the community college. She'll go to University of Washington in the fall, but for the time being, I'm making use of the fact that she's in the same city as me. As I write this book, she pursues her photography. We recently babysat my five-year-old cousin Haley and used her for a photo shoot. She also documented my getting a tattoo over the scars on my arm. I see her often, but use Facebook to keep up with my other close friends, some of whom are away at college and others whom I simply don't have time to hang out with these days. I still don't have a way to see my mother very much, but she's carrying on. Her health isn't much better, but she works from home, writing a mental health column, and she recently worked on a political campaign.

I was emotionally vulnerable after doing research for this

book. I found out things I never knew about my childhood. My childhood memories had always been fuzzy, and when my grandma, mom, and dad filled in the missing pieces, I felt the trauma of a toddler wash over me. Just like my freshman-year vignettes, my sophomore-year writing portfolio, and my junior-year published essay, writing this book has provided catharsis and helped me remain grounded. Parts of each of those writings were put into this book. I think I have found my passion and I don't plan to stop.

I eat healthy, try to exercise, and do my best to get a decent amount of sleep. When my dad lost his job and I lost my insurance, I switched my prescription to Prozac. It's eight dollars for a thirty-day supply and it works. I'm still out of therapy, but I know to ask for help if I need it. When I struggle, I can identify the problem, find a solution if there is one, and let myself feel bad without resorting to unhealthy coping mechanisms. Then I let the happiness in.

Book Club Discussion Questions for HANNAH

1. Hannah tells her story through self-contained vignettes rather than a more traditional narrative way of storytelling. Do you think this approach works for Hannah's story? Why or why not?

2. Hannah's story brings readers inside some of the most painful moments of her life—including two suicide attempts and a rape trial—in a very raw, honest way. Were there any scenes in *Hannah* that were uncomfortable for you to read or that stayed with you after putting the book down?

3. After her first suicide attempt, Hannah spent thirty days in a rehab facility. The doctors recommended a three-month stay, but her insurance wouldn't cover the extra time. Do you think Hannah's story would have been different had she been able to stay at rehab for two more months?

4. Hannah uses a number of strategies she learned in her various therapies to help her cope when things get

overwhelming for her. What strategies did you notice Hannah use throughout the book? Do you have any strategies you use when you are feeling upset, frustrated, or overwhelmed?

5. In the vignette entitled "The Trial," Hannah describes what is going through her mind at the moment she is having a panic attack. Have you ever had a panic attack or known someone who has had one? If so, what was the cause for the panic attack? How did it ultimately subside?

6. When someone commits or attempts suicide, many people in that person's life—friends, family, acquaintances—are impacted and experience guilt for not doing more to prevent what happened. From what you read in *Hannah*, do you think the author's suicide attempts could have been prevented? What signs, if any, were there?

7. In the writing of this book, Hannah made some discoveries about her family that, while giving her clues as to why she is the way she is, were unsettling and upsetting to uncover. Have you ever discovered a part of your family history that has had a negative or disappointing affect on you? If so, how did you handle it?

8. By the end of the book, Hannah ultimately accepts the

diagnosis of borderline personality disorder as the form of mental illness she suffers from. What do you think accepting this diagnosis means for Hannah in her personal journey? Do you think it will help or hurt her? Why?

About the Author

Hannah Westberg is nineteen years old. She earned her GED and plans to enroll in Portland Community College's drug and alcohol counselor certification program. When she's not babysitting, she is probably volunteering for political and charity organizations, as well as participating in flash mobs.

More Louder Than Words Stories

Rae

MY TRUE STORY
of Fear, Anxiety,
and Social Phobia

by Chelsea Rae Swiggett edited by Deborah Reber

Code 5275 • Paperback • $7.95

When you're fourteen and trying to deal with the highs, lows, traumas, and humiliations that go along with being a high school freshman, having severe anxiety can become all consuming. Chelsea Rae Swiggett's anxiety has affected every area of her life—school, family, friendships, and romance—ultimately pushing her to lose her voice, withdrawal from everyday life and school, and develop an eating disorder.

www.louderthanwordsbooks.com

More Louder Than Words Stories

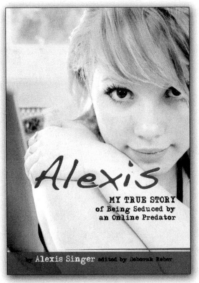

Alexis

MY TRUE STORY
of Being Seduced by
an Online Predator

by Alexis Singer edited by Deborah Reber

Code 5291 • Paperback • $7.95

At the age of sixteen, Alexis Singer was solicited by, manipulated by, and eventually became involved with a married thirty-seven-year-old man over the Internet. He coerced her into having cybersex with him and sending him explicit photos of herself.

In her debut memoir, Alexis Singer describes how she, a bright student at an arts school in Pittsburgh, first encountered an older man on a message board and how he posed as a friend and father figure who could support and advise her when her own father was physically and emotionally absent.

www.louderthanwordsbooks.com